25 MOUNTAIN BIKE TOURS
in the Hudson Valley

25 MOUNTAIN BIKE TOURS
in the Hudson Valley

Peter Kick

A Guide to the Mountain Trails, Back Roads,
Rail Trails, and Carriageways of the Hudson Valley

The Countryman Press
Woodstock · Vermont

An invitation to the reader

Although it is unlikely that the roads you cycle on these tours will change much with time, some road signs, landmarks, and other items may. If you find that such changes have occurred on these routes, please let the author and publisher know, so that corrections may be made in future editions. Other comments and suggestions are also welcome. Address all correspondence to:

Editor, Bicycling Series
The Countryman Press
PO Box 748
Woodstock, Vermont 05091

To Elizabeth and William Kick, my mother and father

Library of Congress Cataloging-in-Publication Data

Kick, Peter.
25 mountain bike tours in the Hudson Valley / Peter Kick.
p.   cm.
Includes bibliographical references.
ISBN 0-88150-360-6 (alk. paper)
1. All terrain cycling—Hudson River Valley (N.J. and N.Y.)—Guidebooks. 2. Hudson River Valley (N.J. and N.Y.)—Guidebooks. I. Title.
GV1045.5.H83K53 1996
796.6'4'097473—dc20   95-39145
                                        CIP

10 9 8 7 6
Printed in the United States of America
Cover and text design by Sally Sherman
Cover photo by Dennis Coello
Interior photos by the author, unless otherwise noted
Maps by Dick Widhu, © 1996 The Countryman Press
Published by The Countryman Press,
    P.O. Box 748, Woodstock, VT 05091
Distributed by W.W. Norton & Company, Inc.,
    500 Fifth Avenue, New York, NY 10110

Acknowledgments

Like many of this era's bicyclists, I owe a debt of gratitude to my parents for getting me started so many years ago with my first "English racer." My parents took my sister and me on long rides over the few extant bike paths of the day, and biking became my primary means of transportation until my late teen years. Later, this early appreciation of the sport became a major recreational outlet for me.

In terms of this book's production, extreme gratitude goes to my wife, June, who shared in most of the rides, picked me up in out-of-the-way places at odd times, and gave up her own cycling time to retrieve me from remote locations. She's the one who assured us of having good lunches and extra supplies, who helped in calling for details and obtaining maps and information, and who entered the manuscript text into the computer (What else is there? you might ask).

Thanks go to my son, Ryan, for his 14-year-old's perceptions of what was boring and what was not and for his enthusiastic riding companionship, as well as for that of Lauren Dellolio, my niece. To William Joseph (BJ) Dellolio, my nephew—a Nyack resident—I am indebted for assistance in researching the tours of that area, as well as for consistent riding companionship. Before my eyes, during the creation of this book, he became a mountain biker.

As for my other riding companions, I thank Larry Kosofsky for aiding in tour layout in the Shawangunks, and Hugh Christie (we both went over the handlebars one memorable day at Ringwood) for suffering long, hot days of exploration. Other test riders figuring heavily in the mix are Tim, Grace, and Will Gifford; Josh Mendez; Susan Christie (thanks also for typing); Craig Furey; Christine Furey; Barbara Hart; Karen Van Vliet; the boys of the Rhinecliff Union Free School District; and the students of the Overlook Mountain Center, as well as its principal, Laurie Griggs. And thanks to Joe and Linda Dellolio for their considerable transportation and support contributions. Also, thanks to Joseph Chernalis for his photographic assistance.

Castle Point, Minnewaska State Park

Thanks must also go to the various people and organizations who assisted my research: Pat Strickland; the librarians of the Nyack Public Library; George Profous, Senior Forester, Region 3 Headquarters; Kenneth G. Krieser, Superintendent, New York Section, Palisades Interstate Park Commission; David Delucia, Director of Parks Facilities, Westchester County Department of Parks, Recreation, and Conservation; Lou Ann Crowley, Club Program, Adventure Cycling Association; the staff of the International Mountain Biking Association (IMBA), Boulder, Colorado; Rob Wrubel, Publisher, *Cycling Times;* the staffs of Minnewaska State Park and Mohonk Preserve; Sheldon Quimby of the D&H Canal Heritage Corridor Alliance; Bernadette Castro, Commissioner, New York State Office of Parks, Recreation, and Historic Preservation; Brian Goodman, Historic Site Supervisor, Old Croton Trailway State Park; John H. Kennedy, former Regional Director, New York State Office of Parks, Recreation, and Historic Preservation, Taconic Region; Bill Bauman, Park Manager, Clarence Fahnestock Memorial State Park; Lynn Bowdery, President, Wallkill Valley Rail Trail Association; John Rahl, owner, Rosendale Section WVRT; The Wallkill Valley Land Trust, owner, Gardiner Section WVRT; Bob Chesterman, Glens Falls Feeder Canal Alliance; Dan Culligan and John Demura, New York State Thruway Department Canal Authority; Mark King, Schenectady County Planning Department; Nonna Shtipelman, Hudson River Sloop *Clearwater,* Inc.; Helen Whybrow, Editor in Chief, The Countryman Press, and Laura Jorstad, Managing Editor, who, through countless letters and late-night phone calls, nurtured both author and text. Her efforts are both (profoundly) evident and appreciated.

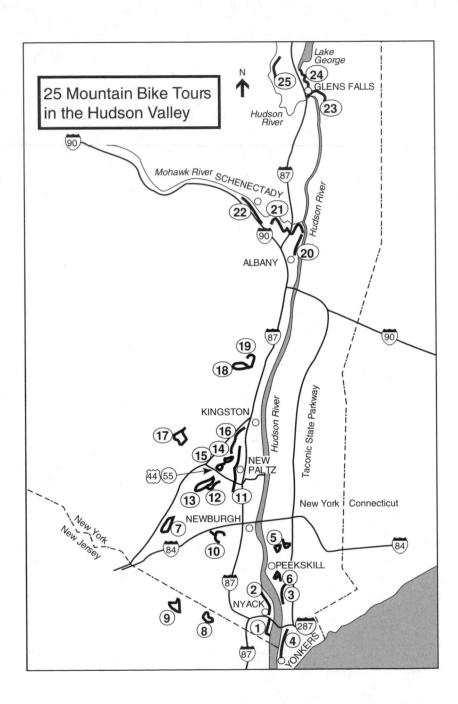

25 Mountain Bike Tours
in the Hudson Valley

Contents

Introduction

Friends of my heart, lovers of Nature's works,
Let me transport you to those wild blue mountains
That rear their summits near the Hudson's wave . . .

From "The Wild," by Thomas Cole

The sprawling headlands, plateaus, foothills, and floodplains of the Hudson Valley have for nearly four centuries attracted the eye and hand of humanity. From prehistoric Indian paths to fur-trading routes, military roads, and, later, railways and canals, inroads to the interior continent were laid out along the valley's most scenic and central corridors. Early settlers and people of commerce could not have helped noticing and appreciating the beauty of their surroundings as they traveled them. The Hudson River, supplying the means of transportation for these early traders, pioneers, soldiers, farmers, and industrialists, took them quickly and inexpensively into the Champlain and Mohawk Valleys, and into lucrative trade with Canada. Trade routes and railroads soon connected the valley's richest bottomlands with the river, leaving the higher ridges to the tenant farmers who scratched out an austere living among the wildcats and rocky fields of the hinterlands, and, later, to the intensive tourist development of the 1800s.

Many of these old roads have become our present-day thoroughfares, overlaid with pavement, their origins erased. Others have remained in memory and name as old post roads, king's (military) highways, settlement roads, county routes, and stage roads that we use every day, in most cases oblivious to the fascinating histories they contain. Still further, beyond the brush and in the densely overgrown and long-forgotten past, many of them eagerly bulldozed aside to make way for new roads and new lives, are the old roads, the railbeds, canalways, towpaths, and foot trails of our early countryfolk. Beyond them, usually on the hills and inland ridges, are the more intact carriage roads of 19th-century leisure America, which have fared better, avoiding the thrust of heavy development and with the aid of state and private preserve protection.

Although we are only recently seeing the rediscovery and appreciation of our environment, the seeds of historic preservation had been sown long before they were acted upon. The transcendental ideals of Emerson and Thoreau are reflected regionally in the works of Washington Irving (1783–1859) and by the earlier lyric poet Philip Freneau (1752–1832). James Kirk Paulding (1779–1860), a contemporary of Irving, praised the environment in his epic poetry and travel guides (*New Mirror for Travelers* and *Guide to the Springs*). Among the post-Knickerbockers, James Fenimore Cooper, William Cullen Bryant, and Thomas Cole (who was also a poet) set the example for a national heritage in praising the Hudson Valley's many assets. Cole's Hudson River School of landscape painters extolled the valley's natural environment, expressing a renewed respect and appreciation for nature. This idea of the godliness of nature had, fortunately, evolved beyond the biblical philosophy that men should subdue nature (a thought held dear by our nation's pioneer men and women, who believed it dark, threatening, and—in the case of our early Dutch settlers—the devil's dwelling place). The transition to the socially accepted philosophy that nature was something to cherish and protect, and that it was not threatening but beautiful, took nearly 2000 years. Sadly, this philosophy seems to have weakened from that bright optimism, and we must constantly stand vigil against levels of desecration, pollution, and destruction of our environment that would have shocked our predecessors.

Largely ignored during the era of post–World War II development, many of our historic routes came to scrutiny as the country picked itself up and began to evaluate its inherent natural endowments. Concurrent with the social revolution of the 1960s, grassroots movements began to penetrate deeply into environmental concerns. People began to take a closer look at themselves, at their forebears, and at their heritage, and to realize the opportunities in historic trails and roadways and the cultural areas these connect. With the generation of federal funding for such projects, the concept of a historic trail system, a greenway, or a heritage corridor began to develop, along with the keen sense of place consciousness that is both our aesthetic legacy and our inalienable right.

Substantial government grants, legislative acts, large endowments of property from families like the Rockefellers and Harrimans, the formation of state and national historic preservation and recreational branches of government, and the efforts of towns, counties, and individuals have

A group of cyclists enjoys a trail along the Hudson River.

engendered a renaissance of trail development in the Hudson Valley. Many of us share a vision that these trails will connect into long scenic greenways on both sides of the river.

Municipalities—encouraged, funded, or otherwise aided by organizations like the Hudson River Valley Greenway Council and Heritage Conservancy and its Model Community Program and Agricultural Advisory Council; the Departments of Transportation, Environmental Conservation, Economic Development, Recreation, and Historic Preservation; and the multitude of privately funded organizations that exist in the valley—have developed local trails and greenways with their neighbors. Their combined interests represent the Greenway Conservancy's mission: the preservation, enhancement, welfare, and prosperity of the natural and historic resources of the Hudson Valley.

Little organizations, supported by citizens such as yourself, are responsible for many of the trails discussed in this book. The Feeder Canal Alliance, the Hudson Valley Heritage Corridor Alliance, the Wallkill Valley Rail Trail Association, Friends of Croton Aqueduct, the Mohonk Preserve—they are all run by small staffs, most of them volunteers. Some have no paid staff at all. The other trails are operated and maintained by large state and county systems like the Palisades Park Commission, the New York State Department of Environmental Conservation, and the towns or counties in which they exist. Most of these agencies are not staffed to provide for the growing interest in off-road cycling and are asking for help. The future development and maintenance of these trail systems will depend more and more on the proactive aspect of the bicycling community.

As you pedal along in the serenity of these trails, listen closely to the echoes of the rich history they represent. Put your ear to the past as you glide along in ghostly silence over the same dirt that families traveled on in their creaking wagons, whose loved ones dashed from their tally-hos and cutters to meet them at the river wharves and backwoods stage stops, whose freight boxes and stone slabs crowded the loading decks of sloops and canal barges while barefoot children led the family mule along the towpaths. Listen—and imagine—and perhaps you'll hear the murmur of their voices among the hand-laid canal stones, singing "Low bridge comin', everybody down." For history is made in layers, and you are among them.

> *I want the Greenway to be an emerald necklace, a legacy.*
> —Mario M. Cuomo

> *To make a Greenway is to make a community.*
> —Charles E. Little, Greenways For America

> *The Greenway will only be successful if it is shaped by the people—the residents of the Hudson Valley.*
> —Senator Jay Rolison Jr.

> *This long tradition of American citizen action applies particularly to the Hudson.*
> —Laurance Rockefeller

Notes for Using This Guidebook

Mileage

For reasons discussed under "Cyclocomputers and Cyclometers," the mile marks in this book must be considered guidelines, not absolutes. They are given in tenths, and in some cases hundredths, of a mile. Don't expect your cyclometer to reflect the book's mile measurements for any given tour. It won't. While my intent is to give an accurate, overall tour distance, the readings for specified turns and landmarks will vary from your own. Accordingly, use the given mileage as a reference, and where it is suggested in the text, carry the appropriate maps and refer to them, as well as to landmarks, for direction finding.

Cyclocomputers and Cyclometers

Cyclocomputers are among the more fidgety and accident-prone gadgets on the accessory list of bicycling. Most mountain bikes on the trails today are not equipped with them. Off-road riders are not as concerned with mileage as touring bikers, and the excessive wiring and wheel- and spoke-mounted hardware is a liability in the brushy, bumpy, brash environment of the off-road cycle. In general, the more expensive and complicated these gadgets become, the less reliable they are. Wireless models may eliminate one distraction, but they usually have a larger fork-mounted sensor-transmitter than wired models. Having this much high-tech mass low down on your fork is not desirable. Also, proximity to whirring machinery (like your car's motor) may drive them wild. Wireless models are also known to interfere with heart-rate monitors and are susceptible to microwave transmission (cellular phones). Thus, new "interference-free" models have appeared on the market.

Speed and distance readings are helpful, but some other cycle computer features are gimmicky and redundant. Maximum and average speed (who cares?), clock and stopwatch (what about your wristwatch?), dual interval timers, training summaries, programmable multiple bicycle calibration, calorie counters, built-in heart-rate-limit warnings (what next?) are all useful training tools but quickly add to the complexity of the ride.

Even a reliable computer is prone to inaccuracies. Differences in calibration when mounting (figuring the correct wheel circumference) as well as surface wheel spin, car-rack wheel spin (take your cycle computer off while traveling), carrying your bike, and forgetting to reset the device will all influence your readings. If you get one, ask your dealer for the simplest, most reliable model—which is usually the cheapest—and let the dealer install it. Then, compare your trip distances with those of friends and maps to see if yours are accurate. If they don't acceptably approximate a map or measured mile, you'll need to recalibrate.

Maps

Many riders wish to explore outside the area shown on this book's maps, and may not find them detailed enough; additional maps are usually suggested in the tour headings. Most of the parks and facilities you visit hand out maps (the maps here are based on these). But maps are not always available, and in many cases they have come directly from the United States Geological Survey (USGS) topographic quadrangles. Many of the regular topo sheets available at sporting goods stores are not updated frequently enough to reflect the trail changes taking place. However, it is always interesting to note the historic and established routes on these maps. They are also considered the best maps for land navigation purposes and represent the only comprehensive mapping coverage of New York State.

You will find that county maps and regional atlases and gazetteers are the most useful aids for getting you to and from tour sites, but normally these don't contain enough detail to be used in the type of land navigation an all-terrain cyclist might find necessary. So if you do plan to get off the trails suggested in the tours, first be reasonably sure you're not venturing onto private property (which should be posted); second,

Author's son, Ryan, trying to delay the inevitable in Vernooy Kill Woods.

have the appropriate USGS map for the area you're riding. These can be ordered from the addresses below, or you can try to buy them near the tour location. If you expect to wander onto lands in proximity to large tracts of forest preserve—where it's possible to get lost for long periods of time—carry a compass and the additional supplies you will need in the event of an emergency.

The best maps for the parks and trails most commonly used by recreationists are the New York–New Jersey Trail Conference maps, which cover most of the Catskills and Shawangunks, as well as several of the other trails discussed in this book. Partly because the organization has been around since 1920, and its founders were responsible for building the first section of the Appalachian Trail (it currently claims to maintain about 1000 miles of trail), the conference takes a very proprietary attitude toward trail use and policy development. In fact, they claim on their 1995 printing of the Catskills map set that mountain bikes are not permitted on any hiking trails, but only on woods roads. There are, however, no laws regulating the use of mountain bikes on state lands in the Catskill Forest Preserve. While the development of such policies is both inevitable and frugal, they don't exist at this time. Nor is it likely that ATBs will be restricted to woods roads when regulations are introduced. Chances are, multiple-use trails such as horse and snowmobile trails (which normally, but not always, traverse something that approximates a woods "road") will be fair game for cyclists, and the higher, more sensitive hiking trails will be off-limits. And that is as it should be. It should be noted that on Tour 19, Old Mountain Turnpike, cyclists are encouraged to use a section of trail that is not a woods road by any means—although it is a horse trail, and it is legal. Several other trails in the Catskills, though they are not discussed in this guidebook, fall into the same category. The best general advice to the mountain biker, considering the fact that plenty of good riding is available for everyone, is to stay off all trails that cannot be classified as multiple-use and wilderness areas.

Conference maps are an indispensable aid to any backcountry user. They contain all sorts of useful information regarding emergencies, bus timetables, clubs, weather, park hours, phone numbers, and history. They are widely distributed and are easier to get hold of, on short notice, than USGS maps. To be sure, order your maps in advance or inquire at your local sporting goods or camping supplies store. More recently, bike shops have begun to carry them and will often prove to be a great source of odd maps, pirated overlays, and standard topographic maps. Ask around. To order maps:

New York–New Jersey Trail Conference (NY–NJTC)
156 Ramapo Valley Road, Mahwah, NJ 07430
201-512-9348

Map Information Unit
Center for Geographic Information
Albany, NY 12232
518-486-1092

Map Distribution Branch
US Geological Survey
Box 25286, Federal Center, Denver, CO 80225
1-800-USA-MAPS

Safety

Many of these tours are in close proximity to vertical drops hundreds of feet high, steep trailside ravines, and high, overhead rock walls. Precipitous and potentially hazardous terrain is home to the mountain bike, but you must exercise discretion to ensure a happy and safe experience. Be especially alert when traveling with children. Be firm and repetitive with them and insist on helmets. (In fact, in New York State, kids 14 and under are now legally required to wear helmets while on bikes.) Ride ahead of them when approaching the potential hazards discussed in the text. Walk when you're near dangerous drops.

Carry a small first-aid kit with several large Band-Aids, a gauze pad, and some antiseptic in your handlebar bag or underseat bag. You yourself wouldn't necessarily apply a Band-Aid to a small cut or abrasion, but kids really like them, and giving them the extra attention will help to maintain morale.

Carry extra food, water, and clothing. If you get lost, have a breakdown, or find yourself delayed for any reason, these items will help. Remember: Bicyclists are susceptible to exposure, too.

Berry-picking on Hamilton Point Carriageway

Tools and Flats

Going afield without tools is risky. You may be in for a long walk for want of just an adjustable or Allen wrench. People walking their bikes in a state of dejection will often ask if you have a certain tool. An excellent, if not mandatory, investment—one that you can shove into your

20

wedge, bar, or frame pack and forget about—is one of the multitools offered by bicycle pro shops and mail-order companies. Some are better than others (you'll discover this someday while trying to extract and replace a chain rivet with an inferior chain tool while sweat drips from your body and mosquitoes assault your back). Buy a good one. They contain (almost) everything you'll ever need "and nothing you don't" for minor trail repairs.

What they won't do, however, is fix flats. You've got to carry at least two tire levers and a patch kit if your tool set doesn't include them (some do). You can carry an extra tube if you want and forget the patch kit. Having a patched tire increases the odds of your having to replace the tube anyway, and spare tubes are cheap. Last, you're going to need a pump or source to air up after a flat. If you know you've got a puncture, you can always add a little "slime" as you reinflate, which seals punctures up to about ³⁄₁₆-inch diameter. Then inflate with either your pump or a CO_2 inflation device. The latter fits any valve, and some handle any size cartridge. Don't expect to achieve perfection on your first try with an inflator, however. It takes a little practice. Until you're good at it, carry extra CO_2 cartridges.

Riding Technique

Read up on climbing and descending if you haven't done so yet. Learn which brake lever operates which brake. Learn about out-of-saddle positions, pedal positions, brake feathering, and "letting go"—gaining enough speed to clear obstacles that would send you over the bars at lower speeds (there are books available on the subject).

Biker's Checklist

Day Trips
full water bottle
cycling shorts
helmet
sunglasses

gloves

first-aid kit

lock

tire repair tools and patches

pump or CO_2 inflator

extra tube

basic tool kit

map

lunch/snack

sunscreen

raingear

Optional but Useful Items (Especially for Longer Tours)

panniers (saddlebags)

handlebar bag

rack strap

headlight/taillight

batteries

journal

camera

towel/swimsuit

windbreaker

International Mountain Biking Association
Rules of the Trail

1. **Ride on open trails only.** Respect trail and road closures (ask if not sure), avoid possible trespass on private land, obtain permits and authorization as may be required. Federal and State wilderness areas are closed to cycling.
2. **Leave no trace.** Be sensitive to the dirt beneath you. Even on open trails, you should not ride under conditions where you will leave evidence of your passing, such as on certain soils shortly after a rain. Observe the different types of soils and trail construction; practice low-impact cycling. This also means staying on the trail and not creating any new ones. Pack out at least as much as you pack in.
3. **Control your bicycle.** Inattention for even a second can cause problems. Obey all speed laws.
4. **Always yield the trail.** Make known your approach well in advance. A friendly greeting (or a bell) is considerate and works well; don't startle others. Show your respect when passing others by slowing to a walk or even stopping. Anticipate that other trail users may be around corners or in blind spots.
5. **Never spook animals.** All animals are startled by an unannounced approach, a sudden movement, or a loud noise. This can be dangerous for you, for others, and for the animals. Give animals extra room and time to adjust to you. In passing, use special care and follow the directions of horseback riders (ask if uncertain). Running cattle and disturbing wild animals are serious offenses. Leave gates as you found them, or as marked.
6. **Plan ahead.** Know your equipment, your ability, and the area in which you are riding—and prepare accordingly. Be self-sufficient at all times. Wear a helmet, keep your machine in good condition, and carry necessary supplies for changes in weather or other conditions. A

well-executed trip is a satisfaction to you and not a burden or offense to others.

—Reprinted by permission of the International Mountain Biking Association (IMBA), PO Box 412043, Los Angeles, CA 90041

SOUTHERN HUDSON VALLEY

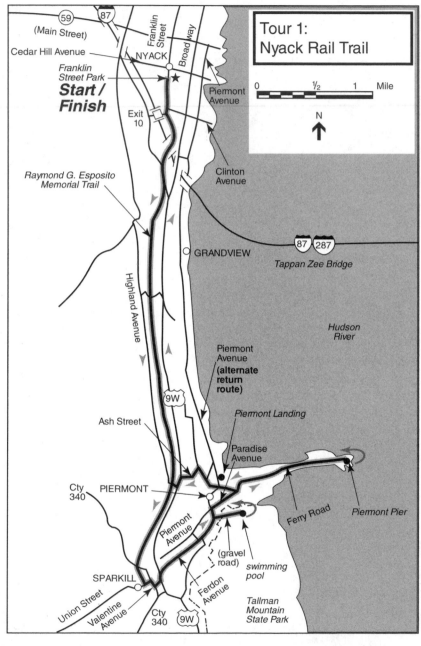

**Tour 1:
Nyack Rail Trail**

0   ½   1   Mile

N
↑

(59) (87)
(Main Street)

Cedar Hill Avenue

Franklin Street

Broadway

NYACK ★

Franklin
Street Park
**Start /
Finish**

Piermont
Avenue

Exit
10

Raymond G. Esposito
Memorial Trail

Clinton
Avenue

GRANDVIEW

(87) (287)

Tappan Zee Bridge

Highland Avenue

*Hudson
River*

Piermont
Avenue
**(alternate
return
route)**

9W

Piermont Landing

Ash Street

Paradise
Avenue

Cty
340

PIERMONT

Piermont
Avenue

Ferry Road

Piermont Pier

(gravel
road)

*swimming
pool*

SPARKILL

Union Street

Valentine
Avenue

Cty
340

9W

Ferdon
Avenue

*Tallman
Mountain
State Park*

1
Nyack Rail Trail

Location: *Rockland County*
Terrain: *Flat with one steep climb*
Distance: *13.1 miles round-trip*
Surface conditions: *dirt, paved*
Map: *USGS Area Topographic Map, Nyack*
Highlights: *Piermont Pier; Piermont Landing; swimming at Tallman Mountain State Park; antiques shops*

This trail follows an old revived railbed through wooded residential areas of Nyack and Piermont. Both towns have experienced a renaissance as scenic and antiquing destinations in the past decade and attract tourists year-round. Because the river roads are the destination of many New York City bicycling clubs, many of these visitors arrive by bike. The roads are generally forgiving, and cyclists can come up from the city under their own power, following the Palisades roads and US 9W. Locals use the rail trail in lieu of walking the village streets, and touring cyclists can manage the surface, which is hard and well maintained. Still, many people don't know about this trail and the quiet, scenic connection it forms between the two towns.

Another attraction just north of Nyack village is the river trail at Nyack Beach State Park, a more isolated and off-road route, with some of the most rugged scenery of the northern Palisades, described in Tour 2. You can combine Tours 1 and 2 and complete them both in a day, for a total distance of 23 miles, but the sights in both Nyack and Piermont may interest you in making two separate visits.

The Nyack Rail Trail begins at Franklin Street Park in Nyack, which is located on the Hudson River at the west end of the Tappan Zee Bridge. Nyack is easily reached by the New York State Thruway and US 9W. Get off the Thruway at Exit 10 if you're traveling north (west) across the Tappan Zee, or Exit 11 if you're going south (east).

From Exit 10 turn right onto Clinton Avenue at the traffic light and go one block, turning left on Broadway. Turn west onto Cedar Hill Avenue, finding Franklin Street Park two blocks up on your left. You can park anywhere in the village of Nyack and reach the park quickly by bike.

If you get off at Exit 11, go left on NY 59 (Main Street), cross US 9W at .4 mile (where NY 59 ends) onto Main Street. Keep going, turning right onto Franklin Street at .8 mile. Cross De Pew Avenue at .9 mile. Turn left on to Cedar Hill Avenue at 1.1 miles. The park is on your right.

0.00 *Head south on the Raymond G. Esposito Memorial Trail. You'll see several aerobic stations along the trail as you cross a few town streets on a cinder surface.*

0.60 *Cross over the NYS Thruway.*

1.00 *Pass a gate and a sign reading* HADER PARK, VILLAGE OF GRAND-VIEW, *and continue south.*

Pass through a residential area with very large trees and views of the Hudson River to the east. The trail is wide enough for two riders to ride side by side here, and the surface continues to be very good.

2.00 *You'll reach a four-way intersection where you'll see another* HADER PARK *sign. Go that way, not to your left.*

The trail width varies in this section. One of the notable features of biking through an ethnic area is all the different aromas you'll notice, especially around mealtime. You're often passing through people's backyards and will see quite a few residents along the way.

2.50 *Cross a small wooden bridge, with chain-link sections over heavily built stone abutments.*

3.30 *You reach Ash Street and continue straight across the road. Don't go downhill on the foot trail to your left.*

There is an old station house, now a private residence, on the west side of the trail before you cross the road. You'll be coming up Ash Street on your return to the rail trail from Piermont, so remember this point. Directly to your left, toward the river, you may be able to see Piermont Landing, which you'll reach soon by following the trail. Don't go down Ash Street at this point.

4.20 *Arriving in Sparkill, you'll come to the four-way intersection of US 9W and County Route 340.*

You can either go across the intersection onto the grassy single-track and reach the village green (visible on your left from this intersection), or take the road. Be careful here; traffic comes sporadically from four directions.

The green in Sparkill is a good place to rest, and there are telephones and stores nearby, but you'll want to spend more of your time in Piermont, only a short distance from here.

4.40 *From Main Street in Sparkill, get on Union Street, which is just across the green to the north.*

4.50 *Reach Valentine Avenue, and go right and downhill slightly.*

4.60 *Turn left onto Ferdon Avenue.*

You'll pass a pond on your left. Ride under the huge steel trestle that supports US 9W, and follow a canal to your left that is the man-made extension of a tidal estuary.

5.40 *Turn right onto a gravel road that is the northern entrance to Tallman Mountain State Park.*

There are no signs, but you'll see a (defunct) hand-operated steel drawbridge on your left and the creek just ahead of you.

This is the way to the Tallman Mountain State Park swimming pool. There are a number of trails in the park that can be explored if part of your group would prefer to keep cycling. Should you want to split up, the village is nearby, as well as the pier. There are also picnic areas within the park that can be reached by going uphill on the road you passed just west of the pool.

5.90 *You'll reach the swimming pool.*

A small fee is charged for swimming. To the north from this point you look out over the Piermont Marsh and Hudson River National Estuarine Research Preserve. The marsh is extensive, and you'll get a better look at it from the pier.

6.50 *Returning to Ferdon Avenue, turn right and cross the estuary, then turn right again, onto Paradise Avenue.*

6.70 *Turn right onto the paved pier road (Ferry Road), and continue to its end.*

7.60 Arrive at the pier.

This is a highlight of the tour and should not be missed! Views up and down the river are extensive. The center span of the Tappan Zee Bridge is just to the north, with the palisades to the left of it. Along the west bank of the river are Hook Mountain and Nyack Beach State Park (see Tour 2). There are picnic tables here and a large concrete pier where people bike, walk, and fish.

The pier once serviced a ferry, and freight was delivered here to supply the Continental Can Company, which stood on the site of the landing and the condominiums you see to the west.

Across the river you can see the towns of Irvington (the location of Sunnyside, the home of Washington Irving), Dobbs Ferry, Hastings-on-Hudson, and Yonkers. On the west side, views farther downriver are blocked by Tallman Mountain. Between it and the pier is Piermont Marsh.

8.60 Arrive back at the main road (Paradise Avenue) and turn right. Turn left immediately to avoid trespassing on the private condominium road.

8.90 Reach Piermont Landing off Piermont Avenue.

Now you can relax and look around in the various interesting shops on the landing itself or in the adjacent village. Take a minute to look at the old steam-driven flywheel that once powered the factory at this site. It was left here because wrecking crews were unable to dislodge it. The dent in the smaller cog is said to be from a wrecking ball, which was damaged in the attempt. The monolith of steel was left alone after that and stands as a shrine to its abandoned industry.

The parklike atmosphere of the landing—with its gazebos, restaurant, benches, and river view—along with the awninged shops along Piermont Avenue, make this location particularly attractive and interesting. Piermont holds seasonal festivals and events and obviously takes a great deal of pride in its status as a model riverfront town. Don't miss it.

It is possible to return to Nyack by following Piermont Avenue to the north, taking it straight to South Broadway and into the village, but I recommend that you return to the trail.

Piermont Pier and the Tapan Zee Bridge

While traffic on Piermont Avenue is surprisingly biker-friendly, the dirt path is more serene and ultimately safer. To regain the rail trail, follow the road that the flywheel is on (nameless at this point), and cross Piermont Avenue (staying on the same road) where it becomes Ash Street. Ride steeply uphill.

9.70 *Arrive at the top of Ash Street and turn right.*

9.80 *Turn hard left on Ash Street and continue uphill.*

9.80 *Arriving at the station house mentioned earlier, turn right onto the rail trail.*

   Now you know the way back to Franklin Street Park and your point of departure.

12.10 *Cross South Broadway.*

12.50 *Cross the Thruway.*

13.10 *Reach Franklin Street Park and the trail's beginning.*

   If you haven't taken the time to see Nyack, turn right here

for two blocks to intersect with South Broadway, then go left 0.5 mile into town. Have a look around at the little antiques and art stores. If you want to ride to Hook Mountain, the location of Nyack Beach State Park, continue straight onto North Broadway. From Main Street in downtown Nyack the park is 2.3 miles. For details, see Tour 2.

Bicycle Repair Services

Piermont Bicycle Connection
215 Ash Street, Piermont, NY
845-365-0900

Nyack Bicycle Outfitters
72 North Broadway, Nyack, NY
845-353-0268

Leo's Bicycle Shop
27 Route 303, Tappan, NY
845-359-0693

West Haverstraw Bicycle Center
146 South Liberty Drive, West Haverstraw, NY
845-947-3237

Congers Bike Shop
107 Lake Road, Congers, NY
845-268-3315

Information

Village of Nyack
North Broadway, Nyack, NY 10960
845-358-0548

2

Nyack Beach State Park ("The Hook")

Location: Rockland County, Town of Nyack
Terrain: Flat to gently rolling
Distance: 10 miles round-trip
Surface conditions: Gravel, dirt (smooth)
Maps: New York–New Jersey Trail Conference Map #4B; USGS Area
Topographic Map, Nyack
Highlights: Outstanding views of the Hudson River and the Palisades

This trail, which winds along the Hudson River on dirt roads and paths, makes an excellent day tour for bikers of all ability levels. It begins at Nyack Beach Park, a small attractive picnic area in full view of the Tappan Zee (Dutch for *shallow sea*). Here, the Palisades surface again—the last visible promontory is in Tallman, south of you—in a series of vertical cliffs that are the best East Coast examples of cliffs formed by lava flows.

This section of the doleritic Palisade Sill and its associated piles of joint-block talus are Triassic in origin, or about 180 to 200 million years old. They are similar in composition and history to rifts in North Africa and the American Southwest. These factors contributed to earning Hook Mountain its National Landmark status in 1980 (the Okefenokee Swamp is one other such landmark; there are about 400 sites nationally).

What you'll notice most about the cliffs, aside from their sheer height, are their odd colors, which range from gray to black to weathered orange-brown. A layer of sedimentary rocks that the lava uplifted is reddish brown. You'll see these rocks in the huge piles of talus at the base of the cliffs and in the construction of the several old foundations built by the Palisades Interstate Park Commission (PIPC).

The park commission was formed in a drive to stop the quarrying

33

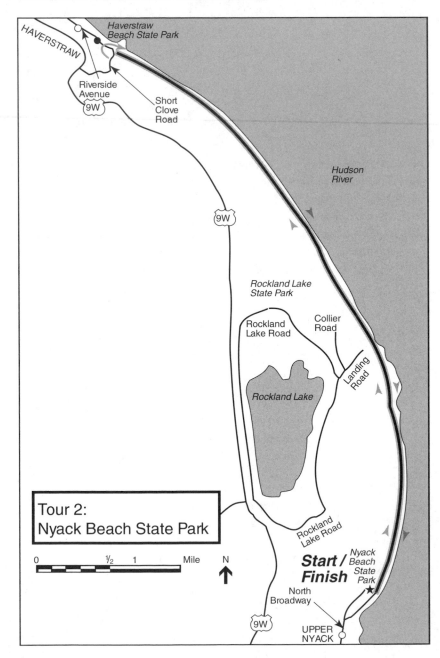

HAVERSTRAW

Haverstraw
Beach State Park

Riverside
Avenue
9W

Short
Clove
Road

Hudson
River

9W

Rockland Lake
State Park

Rockland
Lake Road

Collier
Road

Landing
Road

Rockland Lake

Tour 2:
Nyack Beach State Park

0   ½   1   Mile   N

Rockland
Lake Road

Start /
Finish

Nyack
Beach
State
Park

North
Broadway

9W

UPPER
NYACK

34

and destruction of the cliffs, which peaked around 1872. A quarrying town early on, Upper Nyack supported 31 operations, their docks projecting along the riverfront. Nyack stone was used in the construction of the New York Harbor forts (Castle Williams on Governor's Island, among them), Rutgers College, and the Old Capitol in Albany (1807). The industry moved from freestone quarrying to crushed rock production (the New York Trap Rock Corporation still operates in Haverstraw), and began to eat away the Northern Palisades.

Among those who opposed the quarrying—and ultimately saved the cliffs—was the New Jersey Federation of Women's Clubs. They and others sponsored legislation that resulted in the formation of the Palisades Interstate Park Commission in 1900. As a result, quarrying here and at other locations in the county was halted.

Further development of parks and roads along the Palisades was generated by the Perkins and Rockefeller families and by Mary W. Harriman (former governor Averell Harriman's mother). Her gift of 10,000 acres and $1 million helped create Bear Mountain–Harriman State Park and Hook Mountain State Park. Nelson Rockefeller donated land valued at $10 million.

Several of the park commission's sites allow mountain biking, the most prominent being Minnewaska State Park. Harriman State Park is developing a route.

Nyack is located on the Hudson River, at the west end of the Tappan Zee Bridge. It is easily reached by the NYS Thruway and US 9W. Get off the Thruway at Exit 10 if you're traveling north (west) across the Tappan Zee, or Exit 11 if you're going south (east).

From Exit 10 turn right onto Clinton Avenue at the traffic light, go one block, then turn left onto Broadway. At 0.75 mile north on Broadway you'll intersect Main Street. This is the "antiquing" area of Nyack. Reset your odometer and drive 2.3 miles on North Broadway to the entrance of Nyack Beach State Park. Turn right, go downhill, and park at the river's edge. The trail heads north from the end of the parking lot.

If you get off at Exit 11, go left on NY 59 (Main Street) and straight down to its intersection with Broadway, about 1 mile. (Just one light before reaching Broadway is the right turn onto Franklin Street and the beginning of the Nyack Rail Trail.) Turn left and go 2.3 miles to the park. As ever, be cautious of the large number of pedestrians and children using this area.

0.00 *Head through the gate and bike with the river's edge to your right.*

This section is a flat, dirt road. Due to its exposure the area is often subject to high winds. To your left are huge piles of talus beneath vertical cliffs.

0.80 *Pass a lean-to shelter on your left.*

1.30 *A primitive picnic area with several tables is to your right. Go uphill here on a short section of blacktop road.*

1.50 *Turn right, going downhill. Ride close to the river—back on dirt—past an old foundation on your left. There are river views to the north. Then climb again steeply for a short distance.*

1.90 *Connect with a gravel path.*

This is an old, abandoned section of Collier Road. Uphill, it joins Rockland Lake Road. The steep section you came up was Landing Road, where stone (and ice from Rockland Lake) was loaded onto steamboats and barges. This was Slaughter's Landing, also called Rockland Lake Landing, a regular port-of-call on the river.

Rockland Lake State Park is not accessible by bike from this point, although you could walk there. It is also managed by the PIPC, and there is an attractive paved pathway of several miles' length around the lake.

To stay in the park's good graces, don't ride on the steep Rockland Lake Road if you do go up for a look around.

2.10 *Pass more vertical rock.*

This and most of the level ground beneath Rockland Lake was a huge quarry floor around 1872. The first stone crusher in the area was located near here.

2.50 *The gently rolling trail runs about 50 feet above the river, which widens as you close on Haverstraw Bay.*

2.60 *The trail begins to descend gently. Chain-link fences are placed where the land drops steeply toward the river.*

4.30 *The trail varies in width, but the surface is in excellent condition.*

More cliffs and talus are to your left, many defaced with graffiti.

4.50 *Arrive at a stone barrier with two derelict huts on your right.*

The trail continues on the barrier's north, paved side and climbs.

5.00 The trail ends.

A sign facing north reads CAUTION—HIKERS AND WIDE TIRE BICYCLES ONLY. Wide tires are preferable on this dirt and gravel route, but hybrids and general touring bikes will do well also.

Return the way you came.

This end of the trail is easily reached from Haverstraw at the south end of Riverside Avenue, which can be accessed off US 9W via Short Clove Road.

Bicycle Repair Services

Piermont Bicycle Connection
215 Ash Street, Piermont, NY
845-365-0900

Nyack Bicycle Outfitters
72 North Broadway, Nyack, NY
845-353-0268

Leo's Bicycle Shop
27 Route 303, Tappan, NY
845-359-0693

West Haverstraw Bicycle Center
146 South Liberty Drive, Stony Point, NY
845-947-3237

Congers Bike Shop
107 Lake Road, Congers, NY
845-268-3315

Information

Palisades Interstate Park Commission (PIPC)
Bear Mountain, NY 10911
845-786-2701

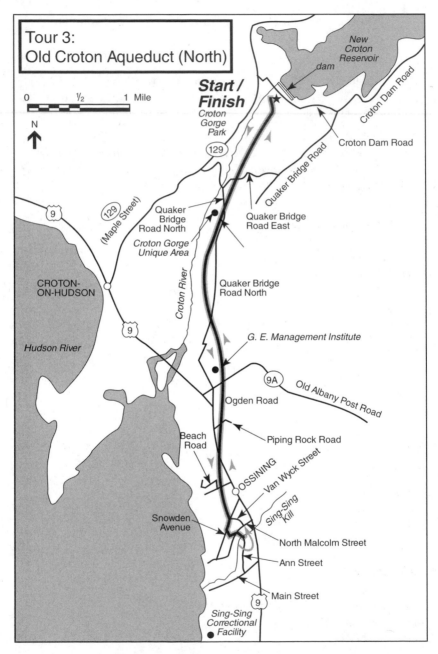

Tour 3:
Old Croton Aqueduct (North)

0   ½   1 Mile

N

Start / Finish
Croton Gorge Park

New Croton Reservoir

dam

129

Croton Dam Road

Croton Dam Road

Quaker Bridge Road

9

129 (Maple Street)

Quaker Bridge Road North

Quaker Bridge Road East

Croton Gorge Unique Area

CROTON-ON-HUDSON

Croton River

Quaker Bridge Road North

9

Hudson River

G. E. Management Institute

9A

Old Albany Post Road

Ogden Road

Piping Rock Road

Beach Road

OSSINING

Van Wyck Street

Snowden Avenue

Sing-Sing Kill

North Malcolm Street

Ann Street

9

Main Street

Sing-Sing Correctional Facility

38

3

Old Croton Aqueduct (North): Croton Dam to Ossining

Location: Upper Westchester County, Town of Cortlandt, access from Croton-on-Hudson
Terrain: Flat to gently rolling
Distance: 10 miles round-trip
Surface conditions: Dirt and cinder trail, carriageway, and occasional road connections and crossings
Maps: USGS Area Topographic Map, Ossining; Upper Westchester County
Highlights: National Historic Landmark; Hudson River Valley Greenway Trail; Croton Gorge Park and Croton Dam; Urban Cultural Park Visitors Center

Also referred to as the Old Croton Trailway State Park, this remarkable bike and foot route follows what has been acknowledged as one of the greatest engineering feats of the 19th century: the Croton Aqueduct. A total distance of 26.2 miles, it was constructed to bring water to New York City in the 1840s, when the lack of water there contributed to prolonged fires and the spread of cholera. Though most of the aqueduct itself is hidden beneath its earthworks or interrupted by modern construction, the remains are sufficient to evoke a feeling for what it once looked like. You can still see the ventilating towers and weir chambers as you pedal along this remarkably attractive and unusual route, most of which is rural or heavily wooded and suburban in character.

This is an ideal trip for families with beginning riders and for seniors and those not up to a strenuous upland tour. It is not a tour that singletrackers seeking side trails or hilly terrain should consider. Efforts to preserve and maintain the aqueduct trail have been strenuous and ongoing, and the people who perform these tasks, both in the various communities through which the trail passes and at the historic site headquarters in Dobbs Ferry, don't appreciate or tolerate misuse or abuse. The trail is owned and managed by the New York State Office of Parks, Recreation, and Historic Preservation, Taconic Region.

As is the case with most linear parks, the lands immediately adjacent to the right-of-way are private. In populated areas such as this you'll also find a large number of people strolling. Because the trail is profusely grass-covered, it is likely you'll startle pedestrians if you're not alert. This is where it's good to have a bell (horns tend to unnerve the unsuspecting).

To reach the trailhead, get off US 9 at Croton-on-Hudson, and turn immediately onto NY 129, heading east. If you don't see any signs in town for NY 129—your cue to exit US 9—follow Grand or Maple Street in an easterly direction, which will lead you to NY 129. At 2 miles, watch closely on your right for a sudden turn into Croton Gorge Park.

Here you'll see the Croton Dam and, to your left, its spillway, both impressive sights, especially at high water when several cascades of wastewater fall from the reservoir. There are comfort stations, picnic tables, a ball field, a jungle gym, and parking. The trail begins here, on the south side of the parking lot, and proceeds uphill. It is not marked at this point. Since the park closes at dusk, you must either return before then or park up above on Croton Dam Road, where the trail can also be accessed immediately south of the dam.

0.00 *Starting from the parking area, go uphill on the cinder road that leads to the trail.*

0.10 *Bear left at a Y, going gently uphill.*

0.37 *Join the trail at a junction, turning right where a sign reads* OLD CROTON TRAILWAY STATE PARK. *Go around the metal pipe barrier.*

Yellow trail markers also appear here, showing the characteristic maple leaf of the Taconic Region trail system.

0.50 *Pass a ventilator in midtrail.*

These structures housed shafts that ventilated the aqueduct, aerated its water, and prevented pressure from developing inside the tube. This section still provides Ossining with water.

0.60 *Pass under a power line.*

1.20 *Cross Quaker Bridge Road East.*

Wooded and residential through this section, the trail here is a wide, grass path with a small strip of dirt worn down its center, most likely from bicycle use. The surface shows little other impact. Confine yourself to the dirt when possible.

1.70 *Cross Quaker Bridge Road North. Pick up the trail immediately on the other side of the road.*

2.00 *You'll enter the 19-acre Croton Gorge Unique Area.*

This area is administered by the NYS Department of Environmental Conservation. The topography is rugged and steep, sloping down to your right (west) into the Croton River.

2.20 *Views toward the Hudson River, where it is met by the Croton, are available here seasonally.*

2.60 *Pass a ventilator.*

2.65 *Cross Quaker Bridge Road North. Regain the trail directly across the road.*

2.95 *At this point the trail is interrupted by the buildings and grounds of the General Electric Management Institute. Turn right here, then immediately left; watch for markers to your right as the trail follows a chain-link fence. Turn right, keeping the fence to your left.*

3.30 *Go right onto Albany Post Road; bear left with the road to pass under NY 9A.*

3.45 *Take a left onto Ogden Road. Ride uphill steeply.*

About 500 feet up Ogden Road follow the trail on your right, passing a maintenance barn and, shortly beyond it, another ventilator. The surface continues to be good here, with the exception of a short but very steep incline. Continue through a residential area.

3.70 *Cross Piping Rock Road, and cautiously descend onto the right-of-way.*

4.00 Reaching US 9, cross diagonally to the left. Use caution.

You'll see signs—and the trail—leading in a southwesterly direction. Continue, passing through the spacious grounds of the Mearl Corporation. You'll feel as if you are on private property, and you are. This is an easement that enables the trail to continue without a detour.

Ride straight across the lawns and onto the path again. There's a small commercial strip to your left on US 9, if you need food, supplies, or a telephone. A seasonal view of the Hudson River exists here.

4.50 Cross Beach Road.

Just before reaching Snowden Avenue, pass a ventilator and waste weir.

4.70 Turn right onto Snowden Avenue.

4.80 As you intersect Van Wyck Street, the trail continues.

4.90 At North Malcolm Street, the trail passes through a small public park with benches and playground equipment. Continue to a stairway and carry or wheel your bike down onto Ann Street.

5.00 You have reached the weir chamber and the location of the Aqueduct Bridge, where it crosses the Sing-Sing Kill.

Weirs were used to divert water from the aqueduct into nearby streams when its carrying capacity was overwhelmed by high water levels or when the interior needed servicing. Tours into the "tube" are conducted on occasion, using weir chambers as access points. This one was constructed in 1882.

You can get a better look at the bridge and the Ossining double arch by taking a small path downhill to a viewing deck, before reaching Main Street.

Both aqueduct and prison memorabilia (including a replica of "The Chair" from the infamous Sing Sing prison nearby) can be seen in the Ossining Community Center's museum. The weir chamber and the Aqueduct Bridge are included in the Ossining Urban Cultural Park. To see exhibits or tour the aqueduct, call the center at 914-941-3189. Tours are frequently scheduled to coincide with the town's street fair, usually held in June.

Biking along the Old Croton Aqueduct Trail

The trail does not end here, but the next several miles include a good deal of convoluted street riding. The section of trail through Rockefeller State Park Preserve is excellent, though short, and cycling anywhere else in the park is unfortunately forbidden. That area is not discussed in this guidebook. Riders wishing to see more of the trail have the southern section, from Lyndhurst to Yonkers, to look forward to.

Return the way you came for a total round-trip distance of 10 miles.

Optional Side Trips

If you want more distance by the time you reach Croton Gorge Park again, there are many attractive roads in the vicinity of the reservoir, Croton Dam Road in particular. Local touring cyclists have mapped out a Croton Dam ride, a hilly 45-miler beginning in Ossining.

The New Croton Reservoir is so large—it joins the Muscoot to the northeast—and is situated in such attractive country, the possibilities for side trips and exploration are as limitless as they are appealing.

Bicycle Repair Services

ET Cycle Center
75 South Riverside Avenue, Croton-on-Hudson, NY
914-271-6661

Sleepy Hollow Bicycles
95 Beekman Avenue, North Tarrytown, NY
914-631-3135

Bikeway
692 Route 6, Mahopac, NY
845-621-2800

Information

Old Croton Aqueduct State Historic Park
15 Walnut Street, Dobbs Ferry, NY 10522
845-693-5259

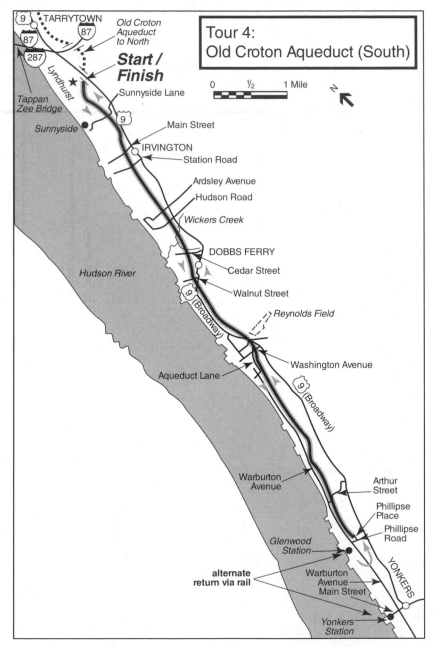

Tour 4:
Old Croton Aqueduct (South)

TARRYTOWN

Old Croton Aqueduct to North

Start / Finish

Sunnyside Lane

0   ½   1 Mile

N

Lyndhurst

Tappan Zee Bridge

Sunnyside

Main Street

IRVINGTON

Station Road

Ardsley Avenue

Hudson Road

Wickers Creek

DOBBS FERRY

Cedar Street

Walnut Street

Hudson River

(Broadway)

Reynolds Field

Washington Avenue

Aqueduct Lane

(Broadway)

Warburton Avenue

Arthur Street

Phillipse Place

Phillipse Road

Glenwood Station

alternate return via rail

Warburton Avenue Main Street

YONKERS

Yonkers Station

4
Old Croton Aqueduct (South): Lyndhurst to Yonkers

Location: Lower Westchester County, access from Tarrytown or Yonkers
Terrain: Flat
Distance: 15.7 miles round-trip (or 9 miles one way with return on Metro North train)
Surface conditions: Dirt and gravel
Map: Lower Westchester County
Highlights: Historic mansions; river views; easy riding in a linear, suburban cultural park; access to railroad for return trip

This is the southern section of the Old Croton Aqueduct Trail, which originates at Croton Dam in the town of Cortlandt. Refer to Tour 3 for background and history.

The two tours vary significantly. The northern half is more secluded and has several stretches of trail with a wild-forest feeling. The trail itself, though frequented by local residents and visited by out-of-town cyclists and walkers, is relatively secluded in its upper realms. The southern half borders on the urban and is populated and busy. You'll see more people using the trail, you'll encounter more traffic at the crossings, and as a result you must exercise more caution. The southern tour changes in character from the elegant and refined grounds of the mansion areas to the built-up ethnic neighborhoods of Yonkers and, for those going farther south, the Bronx.

Here you'll discover the necessity of having a bell or being vocal with strolling pedestrians more than on any other tour in this book.

As you approach Yonkers, the real meaning of the words "urban linear cultural park" will become apparent. Urban cycling will have limited appeal to those who strictly fit the definition of "mountain bikers" and who will be impatient, perhaps, with congestion and crowding when they're accustomed to having most areas to themselves. But for many, the urban linear concept is practical in many ways. This trail in particular offers New Yorkers the chance to escape from the harrowing confinements of city life, ultimately to the countryside, on their bicycles alone. It also offers a convenient and enjoyable alternative to those who wish to commute or simply navigate around large urban environments without using or even owning a car. The health and environmental advantages of this can't be ignored and have constituted a large part of the greenway concept from its inception. This trail, and most of the trails cyclists will encounter or be permitted on in the future, is managed for multiple use. Bikers are only one of the trail's user groups. Be courteous!

For more information on the Old Croton Aqueduct, you can stop by the office as you follow this tour—see mile 3.40—or call 914-693-5259. You might also wish to contact Friends of Old Croton Aqueduct, a nonpartisan, nonprofit educational organization that supports this National Historic Landmark and greenway. They may be contacted at PO Box 131, Hastings-on-Hudson, NY 10706.

For this tour, start in Tarrytown, on the east side of the Tappan Zee Bridge off I-287. Find Lyndhurst, the former mansion of railroad tycoon Jay Gould. The estate is managed by the National Trust for Historic Preservation and is open to the public. It's located on US 9, less than a mile south of its intersection with I-287. Look for it on the west side of the road, just south of the Kraft Foods Technical Center. Cyclists are admitted to the grounds free of charge if they're just passing through. Admission fees to stroll the estate include parking.

If you don't want to pay the Lyndhurst parking fee, it is also a simple matter to find street parking in Tarrytown and ride south on US 9, entering the Lyndhurst property through the second opening in the stone wall, on your right. Set your odometer here, and follow the path west.

0.00 *Enter through the stone wall and immediately come upon a signpost and map. Follow the trail across the open grounds and in front of the mansion; you'll leave the mansion to your right as you proceed.*

Information about touring Jay Gould's estate is available at the gatehouse. Gould was a "robber baron" who sold illegal stocks and bribed politicians in order to dominate the railroads and make millions. He later cornered the gold market, which led to the Black Friday frenzy of 1869.

0.80 *Cross Sunnyside Lane and continue.*

Sunnyside, the former estate of Washington Irving, is to your right, though not visible. Irving bought the property in 1834 and died shortly after its completion, exhausted and in poor health, after finishing *The Life of George Washington*. It can be visited by the public.

Cross several small streets and lanes before reaching Main Street in Irvington.

1.30 *You'll reach the parking lot of the Irvington Middle School. Go straight through the lot and onto the aqueduct across Main Street.*

1.40 *Pass a ventilator shaft. These vents prevented air locks from occurring within the system.*

1.60 *Cross Jewells Brook Culvert, above Station Road.*

Signs here ask that cyclists dismount and walk across the culvert.

2.20 *To your right are Nevis Labs and the Columbia University Press, and just before them, the Octagon House.*

The Octagon (or Stiner-Ross) House is architecturally significant but, unfortunately, private. View it from a distance!

2.30 *Cross Ardsley Avenue.*

2.40 *Pass a ventilator tube.*

2.50 *Cross Hudson Road and, immediately beyond it, pass Mercy College to your right. Continue south into a more residential area. Cross Wickers Creek; climb the hill into Dobbs Ferry.*

3.00 *Cross Cedar Street and go through a parking lot to the left of a restaurant. Follow along past more side streets and parking lots.*

3.40 *You come upon the Old Croton Trailway Aqueduct Office and maintenance buildings.*

Information may be posted here, and there may be personnel available to answer any questions you might have.

The Octagon

Just across Walnut Street is the Overseer of the Aqueduct's House, built in 1845.

3.50 *Cross Broadway.*

The area is densely residential and pedestrians are common. Expect more bikers, joggers, baby carriages, et cetera. The trail is grassy and clean. Cross several roads.

4.65 *A five-way intersection. To your left is Reynolds Field. Cross US 9 diagonally, just southwest of the Episcopal church.*

4.70 *Back on the trailway, continue south.*

4.90 *Cross Washington Avenue onto Aqueduct Lane.*

The trail begins to lose its aesthetic appeal here in spite of river and palisade views to the west.

Pass a series of roads and ventilator shafts.

7.00 *Pass a weir chamber, which is covered in colorful graffiti.*

7.30 *Cross Arthur Street.*

7.85 *Reaching a point where the trail becomes grassy, you can see tall stacks to your right, on the river. You're at the corner of Phillipse Road and Phillipse Place.*

The trail is convenient to Glenwood Station here, should you want to return to Tarrytown on Metro North. The profusion of glass on the dirt trail will discourage you from continuing on it. Many cyclists take to the street here. Those coming from Yonkers north can access the trail from Warburton Avenue or from Yonkers Avenue just west of Dunwoodie Golf Course. The trail officially ends (or begins—if you disregard the direction in which the aqueduct waters flowed) at the northern boundary of Van Cortlandt Park in the Bronx. It can also be accessed from Tibbets Brook Park between the Saw Mill River Parkway and Midland Avenue in Yonkers.

Cyclists choosing to return by rail may prefer the Yonkers station to the more isolated Glenwood stop. It can be reached by going south on Warburton Avenue to Main Street and turning right 1 mile south of the Phillipse corners.

Bicycle permits for Metro North can be purchased from MTA

Metro North Railroad at terminal window #27, Grand Central Terminal, 89 East 42nd Street, New York, NY 10017, for a one-time charge of $5. Applications are available at most stations. Be aware that cyclists are only admitted by conductor discretion, during off-peak hours. For information call 1-800-638-7646.

Bicycle Repair Services

ET Cycle Center
75 South Riverside Avenue, Croton-on-Hudson, NY
914-271-6661

Sleepy Hollow Bicycles
95 Beekman Avenue, North Tarrytown, NY
914-631-3135

Bikeway
692 Route 6, Mahopac, NY
845-621-2800

Information

Old Croton Aqueduct State Historic Park
15 Walnut Street, Dobbs Ferry, NY 10522
845-693-5259

5

Clarence Fahnestock Memorial State Park

Location: *Putnam County, Town of Carmel*
Terrain: *Hilly*
Distance: *Total of 23 miles in two separate loops; 12 additional miles on dirt roads*
Surface conditions: *Dirt horse trails, from smooth to rocky, sometimes steep*
Maps: *New York–New Jersey Trail Conference Maps East Hudson Trails*
Highlights: *Swimming, camping, boating on state park grounds; fine off-road cycling in a variety of settings*

Excellent mountain biking exists at Fahnestock, and more is planned for the future. As of this writing, the area is just being discovered by cyclists, so most of your time on the trail will be spent in solitude. It is suited for intermediate to advanced riders.

At 6532 acres, the park is bigger than most. Also managed by Fahnestock—which is operated by the Taconic Interstate Park Commission—are nearby parcels including Hudson Highlands State Park (which does not have provisions for mountain bikers) and the adjoining Hubbard-Perkins Conservation Area. This huge tract, just northwest of Fahnestock Park, is owned by the Open Space Institute and is the subject of acquisition efforts by the park commission. Of interest to cyclists is a remote trail through the interior of Hubbard-Perkins that is now being developed by the New York–New Jersey Trail Conference for multiple-use purposes.

Conference volunteers share the concern of many hikers that overuse of trails by bikers may diminish the quality of the hiking experience for others. They realize that the creation of multiple-use trails will give cyclists and equestrians nonconflicting places to enjoy their sport. However,

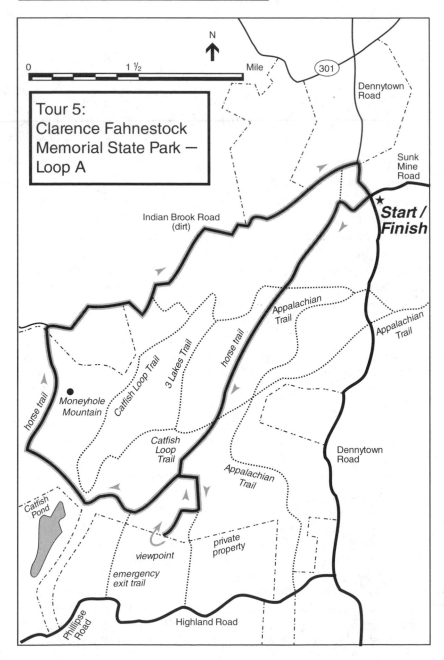

N

0   1 ½   Mile

301

Dennytown
Road

Tour 5:
Clarence Fahnestock
Memorial State Park —
Loop A

Sunk
Mine
Road

★ **Start /
Finish**

Indian Brook Road
(dirt)

Appalachian
Trail

Appalachian
Trail

3 Lakes Trail

Catfish Loop Trail

horse trail

horse trail

Moneyhole
Mountain

Catfish
Loop
Trail

Appalachian
Trail

Dennytown
Road

Catfish
Pond

viewpoint

private
property

emergency
exit trail

Phillipse
Road

Highland Road

54

the conference is leaving the maintenance of these trails to the groups that use them. Since the conference already has so many trails to maintain, including the Appalachian Trail, it only makes sense that bikers share some of the responsibility. Besides, wouldn't you like to ride trails where you don't have to fear colliding with hikers?

To reach Fahnestock from the Taconic State Parkway—the easiest access—get off at NY 301 West, heading toward Cold Spring. The park is immediately west of the parkway.

Access is also simple from the NYS Thruway and I-84. Leaving the Thruway at Newburgh (Exit 17), take I-84 east across the Newburgh-Beacon Bridge. Continue on I-84 for about 5 miles to US 9. Head south on US 9 (from Wappingers Falls) for about 10 miles. Just south of Philipstown, take NY 301 east, from McKeel Corners.

The first loop begins off Dennytown Road, a right turn just under 3 miles east from US 9, or 3.5 miles west (a left turn) from the Taconic State Parkway, on NY 301. Turn onto Dennytown Road, passing Indian Brook Road (also called Stow and Stoe Road) on your right at 0.5 mile. A little beyond (0.2 mile) on your left is a large parking area, adjacent to the seasonal Sunk Mine Road. Just across Dennytown Road from the parking area you'll access the horse trail, which is sparsely marked with small yellow disks.

Loop A: Moneyhole Mountain Bike Trail

0.00 Enter the woods on the horse trail, on the west side of Dennytown Road.

This is an attractive trail; there are some rocks. Stay off the small footpaths to your left (at 0.25 mile).

0.35 Turn left at a T.

The righthand turn would take you back to Indian Brook Road near the parking lot.

0.65 Intersect with the (blue) 3 Lakes Trail. Keep off!

1.10 Pass a trail to your left, which connects with the Appalachian Trail (AT). Continue straight.

1.80 Go straight through the (red) intersection with the Catfish Loop Trail. Continue into a mature pine forest.

1.85   Reaching a Y, turn left.

2.15   Go right at a Y. A smaller trail heads left here, out of the park and onto private property and Highland Road; do not use it.

2.45   The trail dead-ends at a point with an exceptional view of surrounding hills and fields, from Mount Beacon (the one with the towers) south. An old chimney here with a crude fire ring makes an excellent lunch/rest stop. Return to the Y in the pine forest.

3.00   Go left at the Y in the pines.

3.30   Watch carefully to your right; then go sharply right, nearly doubling back on your direction of travel, at a three-way intersection.

     Don't go straight ahead, because the trail reaches Phillipse Road, the west end of Highland Road, within 0.5 mile. It is private property leased by the Garrison Fish and Game Club. Use this trail for emergency egress only.

     Go uphill through thick laurel cover and level out; then drop downhill gently.

4.00   As you come downhill, curving slightly to the left, you reach a point where a vague footpath goes to your right. Bear left! This footpath connects with the (red) Catfish Loop (no bikes). Some red markers appear a short way down that trail if you're uncertain of your location and need to check it.

     Continue on the horse trail, which has no markers through this section. This section, the northern source of Catfish Pond, is slightly muddy. Pay no attention to the posted signs; they'll confuse you. (Some of them have been misplaced on park lands.)

4.30   Make a 90-degree right turn. This turn is not marked. The trail that goes straight hooks around the northwest side of Catfish Pond onto private lands. Catfish Pond is to your left, though in leaf-out you can't actually see it.

     Continue on the horse trail now, gaining elevation as you approach the long ridge of Moneyhole Mountain (900 feet). Your present elevation is 700 feet.

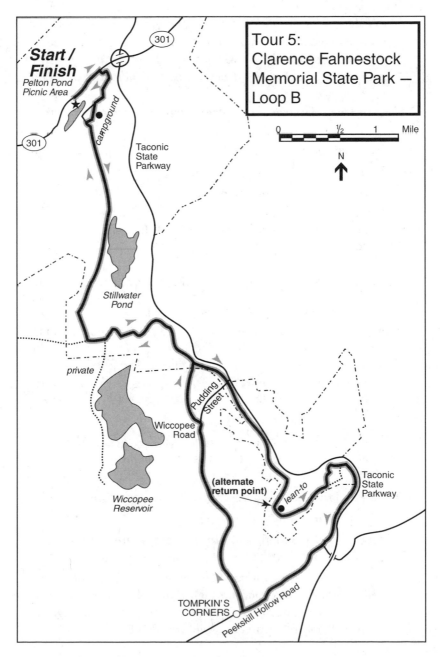

**Start /
Finish**
Pelton Pond
Picnic Area

301

301

campground

Taconic
State
Parkway

Tour 5:
Clarence Fahnestock
Memorial State Park —
Loop B

0   ½   1   Mile

N

Stillwater
Pond

private

Pudding
Street

Wiccopee
Road

Wiccopee
Reservoir

**(alternate
return point)**

lean-to

Taconic
State
Parkway

TOMPKIN'S
CORNERS

Peekskill Hollow Road

The trail is narrow, dirt, rocky, and grassy. It rates highly as a mountain singletrack. Some trail maintenance is needed, as the area is subject to blowdowns and deadfalls. If you wish to backtrack to your car on trails instead of Indian Brook Road (dirt), turn around now.

A steep descent of 0.3 mile brings you to Indian Brook Road.

5.40 *Turn right on Indian Brook Road.*

7.50 *Turn right onto Dennytown Road.*

7.70 *Arrive back at the parking area.*

Loop B: Stillwater Pond Bike Trail to Peekskill Hollow Road

This loop is similar to Moneyhole Mountain but tends to have wider, flatter stretches of trail.

It begins from the park campground, 3 miles east of Dennytown Road on NY 301. If you have just finished the Moneyhole Mountain tour, come out of Dennytown Road and turn right. Park at the Pelton Pond picnic area, 3 miles from Dennytown Road. There are phones and Sani-Jons here. You'll have to ride NY 301 for 0.4 mile west, on a 2-foot-wide tar shoulder, at the beginning and end of this loop.

0.00 *From Pelton Pond picnic area, ride right on NY 301 west.*

0.40 *Turn right into the camping area, pass the check-in booth, go uphill bearing right, and pass the maintenance headquarters to your left.*

0.60 *Pass an information board and toilets to your right.*

0.75 *Pass a water tower to your right.*

1.00 *Reaching a Y, turn left at white markers where signs say* EMERGENCY ROAD—DO NOT BLOCK *and* NO MOTOR VEHICLES.

1.10 *Pass the horse trail parking area on your right. Continue on a well-maintained dirt road through attractive hemlock and laurel forests. The undulating path is never difficult but begins to get rockier as you approach Stillwater Pond.*

1.60 *Appearing on your left is Stillwater Pond (elevation 895 feet). Proceed over increasingly rocky and hilly terrain along its west side. Cresting a rise at 1000 feet, go downhill to a vague T, at a large boulder in the trail. An unmarked trail veers to the west here. This is easy to miss, but unimportant.*

3.17 *Bear left at the T and the large boulder.*

3.35 *Reaching a Y in the trail, head left. The right fork is level and leaves the park to follow the western shore of the private Wiccopee Reservoir.*

Go uphill, cresting the rise, and downhill (southeast), keeping the parkway to your left. The trail is smoother now, and follows downhill into open forest. There are horse trail markers here.

4.45 *In view of a private residence, bear left around the south side of a wet depression (the parkway will be to your left as you reach Wiccopee Road). Bear right onto Wiccopee Road.*

4.50 *Go left onto the bridle trail. The trail is rough here—it was groomed by a bulldozer—but soon improves.*

4.90 *Cross Pudding Street. Bike a wooded area on a wide singletrack.*

5.40 *The trail pulls away from the parkway into a quiet section of forest.*

5.90 *Reaching a well-preserved stone lean-to, you are now at the south end's highest point—900 feet—and will begin to descend to 450 feet over the next mile. This following descent is a very attractive trail, but it is a climb to return over. If you don't want to ride the suggested road miles to loop back to Wiccopee Road (a total of 3.4 miles), you can turn around now.*

The trail switches back to the northeast here and begins with a mostly level, sometimes slightly uphill, profile. But it soon descends, heading south through a hemlock forest as it once again nears the parkway. The last 0.5 mile is a gravel reconstruction.

7.70 *Turn right onto Peekskill Hollow Road (the parkway is to your left). It's shoulderless but not too busy—a fairly mellow country road. It is not, however, recommended for children or those*

not accustomed to riding in traffic. There is bail-out space to
your right if you need to pull over.

8.90 Turn right at Tompkin's Corners onto Wiccopee Road. Go
uphill. Bear left at the intersection with Pudding Street.

11.20 Reaching the end of Wiccopee Road, regain the bridle path
and head north (left), returning the way you came.

15.70 Finish at the Pelton Pond picnic area.

For additional touring at Fahnestock Park, don't overlook Sunk
Mine Road (gravel) next to the Dennytown Road parking area,
where you parked for Moneyhole Mountain Loop. As of this writing, the road is open to vehicles April through November, but it
may be closed in the future. This 6-mile-long road passes John
Allen Pond, in a very scenic area of the park. If you are not an
aggressive mountain biker, you might prefer this to the dirt trails.
It makes an interesting 12-mile round trip. Avoid the side trails
and posted areas.

Bicycle Repair Services

Village Bicycle Shop
97 Old Route 6, Carmel, NY
845-225-5982

Bikeway
692 Route 6, Mahopac, NY
845-621-2800

Information

Clarence Fahnestock Memorial State Park
1498 Route 301, Carmel, NY 10512
845-225-7207

6

Blue Mountain Reservation

Location: Westchester County, Town of Peekskill
Terrain: Hilly
Distance: 6 miles
Surface conditions: Dirt, single- and doubletrack
Maps: USGS Area Topographic Map, Peekskill; Upper Westchester County
Highlights: Spitzenberg Hill; public swimming and picnic area; classic all-terrain riding, easy access

It's unusual to find a county park with the resources and easy accessibility of this excellent biking area. Cyclists will be surprised to find that upon entering the park, they are issued a bike map—"Mountain Bike Trail, Blue Mountain Reservation"—and are greeted with a series of trails with several marked access points displaying the International Mountain Biking Association (IMBA) logo and rules.

While trails have in the past been marked in multiple colors, with old trail signs contradicting more recent ones, a re-signage of the park is being conducted. The map does, however, prove trustworthy, and a good, challenging ride can be had in this well-conceived trail system.

In spite of the marking and maintenance work the park currently faces, it is way ahead of its time in both attitude and preparation for bikers. Very few county or state parks, even when they allow off-road bicycles, are able to offer a map for their exclusive use. Most are still handing out a hiker's map accompanied by verbal guidance as to "which trail to take." The drawbacks of this practice are easily seen in the level of hiker/biker animosity and the amount of peripheral overuse or abuse caused by undermanaged cyclists. Fortunately, all of this is changing rapidly.

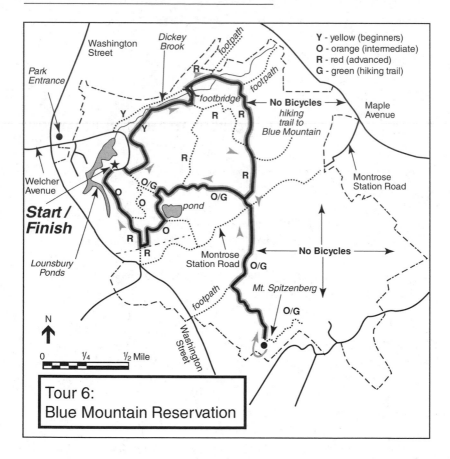

Tour 6:
Blue Mountain Reservation

County park personnel at Blue Mountain, whose numbers have been restricted by the same budget cuts that have stunted the growth of cycling management in many state parks, are planning for tight management of bicycle use in the reservation. The trails, which are Westchester County's "first and only . . . designated primarily for moutain biking" (see map handout), total at least 7 miles and will be marked by skill level: yellow, beginners; orange, intermediate; red, advanced. Any capable biker with experience can manage the trails, but less aggressive riders or children may be daunted by the frequent climbs. Because the topography is low and the trails are former maintenance, fire, and equestrian routes, inclines are neither extreme nor prolonged, with the exception of the last pitch on Spitzenberg Hill, which must—and should—be walked. There is, however, plenty of challenging terrain here, and if ever there was a model county park for off-road cycling research and development, this is it. Remember, the park is still open to hikers and equestrians. Yield trail to both groups. The park is open 7 days a week from dawn to dusk. A parking fee of $6 can be reduced by the purchase of a park pass, though these are for county residents only. After 3:30 PM there is no charge for entering through the main gate. It's possible to park at several access points and ride in without charge or penalty—such as on the west end of Montrose Station Road or in the town of Peekskill itself, just outside the main entrance—but you'll be far from your car. You'll also be forgoing the chance to support the park's efforts to provide you with great biking. Eventually, this type of monitoring and accountability loss may lead to the introduction of annual permit systems and volunteer bike patrols like the ones being developed in larger state parks. Bikers may sometimes find themselves mouthing the familiar rationalization, "Hikers don't pay to walk in, so why should I pay to ride in?" The answer is complex and many-faceted but obvious. In general, there is little argument that hordes of cyclists create environmental impacts (admittedly, this is true of hikers, too—but to a lesser degree). This must be followed up with a regular maintenance program. Bikers need to take some responsibility for that if they expect to gain acceptance. Blue Mountain Reservation is on the threshold of resolving this situation. For information call Blue Mountain Reservation at 914-737-2194 or the Westchester County Department of Parks, Recreation, and Conservation at 914-593-PARK.

The park is simple to reach. Take the Welcher Avenue exit from US 9 in Peekskill. Traveling east, in less than 0.5 mile you'll reach the entrance. Pick up a map and pay the parking fee, bear left, and continue for about 0.5 mile to the end of the road. You'll see several trailheads with businesslike signs posted in front of each.

Start from the trailhead in the middle of the parking lot on its wooded (east) side. Before getting on the trail, read the Cyclist Responsibility Code, based on the National Off-Road Bicycling Association (NORBA) and IMBA codes.

Remember to yield to pedestrians and horses.

0.00 *Enter the woods going slightly uphill, following orange/green on the map. The surface is dirt.*

0.10 *Go left.*

> The terrain is flat now, the forest is extremely dense, and the trail is shaded.

0.60 *You'll come within earshot of a brook and ride up close to it thereafter.*

0.65 *Reach an intersection. A trail to the left crosses Dickey Brook. Go straight.*

0.73 *Turn left at a fork (yellow on map).*

0.87 *Cross a small footbridge.*

0.90 *Turn right on the other side of this bridge at a T with several trail signs and blazes in varying conditions (the sign in the best condition here is the NO BICYCLES sign).*

1.00 *A footpath to your left—which looks bikable and obviously has been used by cyclists, perhaps to access the park from the north—goes northeast to the Cortlandt and Peekskill town lines. Ignore this path and go downhill and cross Dickey Brook again. Proceed uphill.*

1.25 *Turn right at a Y (the map color indicates red) and go steeply uphill. You'll cross a series of rises. The forest cover is dense, there are several large rock outcroppings, and the trail is rocky and wide.*

1.65 *Pass a footpath on your left.*

1.70 *At a Y-junction, go right.*

> The left-hand trail goes uphill over rocks and soon becomes unmanageable; it climbs Blue Mountain (elevation 680 feet) and is closed to bicycles.

1.95 *Pass a vague singletrack on your left. Keep going straight. The trail goes downhill over a rocky, dirt surface.*

2.10 *The trail enters an open area.*

> *Cross Montrose Station Road here to pick up the Spitzenberg Trail. The trail you're leaving continues, going back into the woods. You'll pick it up again later, after returning from Mount Spitzenberg.*
>
> *If you want to take a side trip, Montrose Station Road is*

Pausing over Lounsbury Ponds

dirt and offers a break from rock hopping. Unfortunately, from here it's downhill in both directions. It turns to pavement 0.8 mile to your right on Washington Street, and does the same at 0.7 mile to your left as it exits the reservation.

From your present location, pick up the (orange/green) trail to Mount Spitzenberg directly across Montrose Station Road. Proceed uphill over a good surface.

2.65 At a Y, bear left.

3.10 Arrive at Mount Spitzenberg.

You can walk or carry your bike up to the summit (or leave it at the base, but lock it), which is a short distance from the (ridable) trail. Beyond the stone foundation on the summit is a rock with good views of the southwestern valley.

Return to Montrose Station Road.

4.00 Upon reaching Montrose Station Road, get back on the (orange/green) trail, which will take you through woods on an old dirt road.

4.30 At a T, go left. The trail goes downhill.

4.70 At another T, go left again.

4.85 Pass a pond to your left.

There's a crude campsite here and a view of the pond.

4.95 At a T, go right. (The left—red—trail goes to Montrose Station Road.)

5.10 Breaking out into a narrow meadow, watch on your left for another red trail, which you should see almost immediately. Follow the red paint.

5.20 Cross a gas pipeline right-of-way. You'll recognize this by the large swath of cut-over land and the yellow posts in the ground. Follow red paint blazes.

5.30 You'll see the road coming up in front of you. Follow sharply to your right before reaching the road, staying on the red trail (red paint blazes appear with regularity from now on).

5.40 Recross the pipeline right-of-way and turn left, going downhill.

In about 200 feet, the red trail enters the woods on your right. Continue on it.

5.70 *Cross a wide grass right-of-way and go back into the woods, an area of second-growth timber and stone walls.*

5.95 *At a T, go left.*

6.10 *Continue going straight, passing a trail to your right that returns to the parking lot.*

6.20 *At another T, go right. A gravel path goes left over a steel bridge. Beyond it are playing fields and access to Washington Street.*

6.35 *You'll see Lounsbury Ponds and the parking area. Return to your car.*

The area around Lounsbury Ponds is open to biking at this point, but be careful. Small children play here, and the picnic area is extensive and well used. Cyclists should restrict themselves to the dirt path of the reservation and leave this area to the pedestrians, with the exception of the pond roads that connect the parking areas.

Bicycle Repair Services

Village Bicycle Shop
97 Old Route 6, Carmel, NY
845-225-5982

Bikeway
692 Route 6, Mahopac, NY
845-621-2800

Information

Westchester County Department of Parks, Recreation, and Conservation
19 Bradhurst Avenue, Hawthorne, NY 10532
Reservation: 914-737-2194; County Office: 845-593-PARK

SOUTHEASTERN HUDSON VALLEY

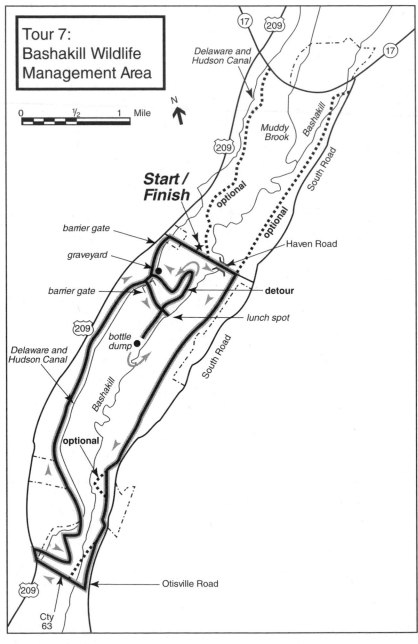

Tour 7:
Bashakill Wildlife
Management Area

0   ½   1   Mile

N

Delaware and
Hudson Canal

Muddy
Brook

Bashakill

South Road

*Start /
Finish*

optional

optional

barrier gate

graveyard

Haven Road

barrier gate

detour

209

lunch spot

bottle
dump

Delaware and
Hudson Canal

Bashakill

South Road

optional

Otisville Road

209

Cty
63

70

7

Bashakill Wildlife Management Area

Location: Town of Wurtsboro, Sullivan and Orange Counties
Terrain: Flat
Distance: 9 miles (with an optional 6+ miles of detour)
Surface conditions: Unimproved railbed, dirt, gravel, grass towpath
Maps: Sullivan and Orange Counties; USGS Area Topographic Map, Wurtsboro
Highlights: Delaware and Hudson Canal and towpath remnants; rich wildlife habitats; scenic touring with singletrack detours

This is a loop tour with optional legs and detours. It represents an unusual opportunity to enjoy southeastern New York's largest freshwater wetland. If you plan to do this tour, it is advisable to write ahead for the New York State Department of Environmental Conservation's circular and map covering this area (see the Introduction). Presently, there is no on-site staff or information.

One of the many remarkable features of cycling in the Bashakill is the intact, well-preserved section of the Delaware and Hudson Canal you'll ride. Now a National Historic Landmark, the canal was abandoned in the early 1900s. Much of it is broken and privately owned, but several long stretches have been restored, primarily in Sullivan, Orange, and Ulster Counties. Private groups and municipalities are taking an active role in its preservation and development for multiple use.

The canal was completed in 1828, primarily for shipping coal to the Hudson River. The Wurtz brothers (for whom Wurtsboro is named) discovered huge deposits of anthracite in Pennsylvania and hired 2500 men to hand-build the 108-mile-long ditch. Beginning in Honesdale, Pennsylvania, and ending in Eddyville on the Rondout Creek, the canal and its adjacent towpath—from which teams of horses, or more frequently mules, pulled barges—are still intact for many several-mile-long stretches. If you like rail trails, you'll like towpaths even more. They tend to be curvier and generally have greater character than railbeds, creating more of a historical, topographical, and architectural puzzle. In several spots along the canal you'll find an adjacent rail trail, but in the case of Bashakill, the railroad bed is on the wetland's east side. You get to ride both.

Several canal museums and newsletters exist for the enthusiast; the local one is the Neversink Valley Area Museum (914-754-8870), PO Box 263, Cuddebackville, NY 12729. The museum is open Thursday through Sunday, noon–4 PM, March through December 22. Along with canal relics and memorabilia, it provides tours, videos, a gift shop and bookstore, a place to walk and picnic on a section of towpath, and, for those familiar with the "charmed circle" of trout fishing creeks, direct access to the Neversink, once a feeder river to the D&H Canal. This was the site of an aqueduct built by John A. Roebling, whose cable suspension designs modernized bridge building and were later used in the Brooklyn Bridge, which he also designed. In 1869, Roebling died in an accident on the Brooklyn Bridge and never saw it completed.

The whole impression of this 2200-acre wetland is that of an Adirondack flow—large, forested, reedy, with islands and backwaters, profuse with bird life and waterfowl, for which this area is managed.

Including the allowed bikeways, the area has 15 miles of foot trails, several observation towers, and boat launch sites, and it provides opportunities for such activities as hunting, trapping, canoeing, and research.

Bluebird and wood duck nesting boxes, as well as osprey nesting platforms, have helped maintain a high level of species diversity. You'll be impressed with the quantity of visible life. Be very careful to stay on the trails to avoid any habitat destruction.

The Bashakill Wildlife Management Area is accessible from I-209 and NY 17. For access from the New York State Thruway, get off at Newburgh (Exit 17) and go west on I-84 to NY 17 North (the "Quickway"). Get off NY 17 at Wurtsboro, and go south on I-209. At 2.2 miles, watch for Haven Road on your left (east). Park at the designated parking area 0.4 mile down Haven Road.

You can also reach the area easily by taking NY 17 north from the NYS Thruway at Harriman or Suffern, getting off at Wurtsboro.

If you are coming from the south on I-209, look for Haven Road at

7.7 miles north of Cuddebackville. Turn right to the parking area.

At the Bashakill Wildlife Management parking area, you'll see state signs. A red foot trail can be accessed here, but since this section of trail is suitable only for hiking, don't take it. Instead, get on the road and head southeast, to cross the kill (the word is from the Dutch, meaning creek or channel) and the Haven Road Bridge.

0.00 *Leave the Haven Road parking area, heading southeast— toward the wetland—on Haven Road. You can see open water and the bridge from here.*

0.25 *Cross the bridge.*

0.45 *Turn right across the street from a parking area. The rail trail runs north-south through here.*

Surface preparation on the railbed has been negligible—the ties are still in place. However, they have decayed to the point that, although they're noticeable and a little annoying in spots, the bed is ridable, and the surface will improve as the ties age and break down. These conditions vary as you head south.

The kill opens up on your right, and you pass through large open sections of wetland. You'll get the feeling of riding on a causeway, with swamps to your left and the widening channel to your right. You'll see birds, ducks, and perhaps an occasional snake (proceed with caution—there are copperheads in the area) as you bump over roots and ties in low gear.

The berm—the raised section of the railbed—is hemmed with white birches. You'll travel in and out of wooded sections.

1.75 *Reach a boating access site.*

2.10 *A trail intersects to your right. This area can be explored. Continue on the railbed, which deteriorates somewhat. Keep on going; it will improve.*

2.30 *The trail intersects a parking area. The railbed has become narrow, and the ties have disappeared through this section. There may be blowdowns or other obstacles such as grown-up brush.*

You'll draw close to Otisville Road now. The railbed loses its width and becomes a foot trail. It stays between the kill and continues south, widening again.

73

3.25 *Reaching a point only a few feet from the kill, you'll find a spring coming up near the trail, almost at lake level. The road is immediately to your left. It's possible to short-cut the remainder of the railbed here by taking the road south to County Route 63.*

3.45 *Pass a parking area on your left. Exit the railbed here (at 3.60 it dead-ends at a southern branch of the kill), and turn right onto Otisville Road.*

3.90 *Pass another parking area, on your right, and immediately turn right onto County Route 63 (also called Indian Orchard Road). Go straight.*

4.30 *Turn right onto I-209. This is a short stretch of not-so-pleasant road. Stay to the right and use caution.*

4.90 *Turn right onto an unmarked road that may have an old state trail sign designating a BOAT LAUNCH area. This road takes you into an open field. Don't go all the way to the kill; instead, watch on your left for an unmarked trail, which is wide enough for a vehicle.*

5.10 *Turn left (north), crossing open fields until you see the towpath berm just inside the tree line.*

5.25 *Walk up onto the berm and turn right onto an excellent dirt doubletrack surface.*

Follow this through the woods with increasingly good views of the Bashakill to your right. The trail's surface ranges from grass to gravel. You may notice red DEC trail markers.

6.25 *A singletrack to your right provides exploration but leads to a dead end. Continue on the towpath.*

Some of the canal's walls are still intact and may contain standing water, profuse with skunk cabbage. Pass a home along this stretch.

6.85 *Cross a wooden bridge.*

7.10 *Pass an old bridge abutment.*

7.20 *Cross another wooden bridge.*

8.00 *Pass a parking area with logs defining its perimeter on your right.*

8.35 *You'll reach an intersection. To your left are two dirt trails, one an unexplored singletrack heading southwest, the other a wide path. The canal is broken up here and not evident.*

The Bashakill from the railroad bed

An old graveyard is just ahead (1840–1870). To your right is a barrier gate and a very ridable detour—a series of pine-wooded trails with a grass-and-moss surface. Once wide enough for a Jeep but now overgrown, they are excellent for cycling. At this point, should you choose to detour, there are directions at the end of this tour description.

From the intersection, follow the wide dirt path to your left.

8.65 *Reaching a barrier gate on a dead-end side road off I-209, go right.*

8.85 *Go right onto Haven Road to your car.*

Optional Detour

0.00 *Leave the intersection, turning right past a barrier gate.*

0.75 *At a four-way intersection, turn right.*

1.20 *Arrive at a dead end, where there is an old bottle dump. Return to the four-way intersection.*

1.70 Go right. Reach a romantic, private lunching spot next to the water, covered in bluets. Return to the four-way intersection.

1.85 Go right, around a pine forest loop and back up to the graveyard.

2.60 Arrive at the first intersection near the barrier gate.

Further Exploration

If you like this area and are interested in touring the north end, you can get additional mileage on the rail trail going north, across the street from your starting point on the southeast side of the kill.

The bed is in better condition, generally, than the south end, and there are a few side trails to be explored. The railbed continues off state land and onto a privately posted segment at 2 miles. Since there is no practical way to cross the area's north end to make a loop back to Haven Road without considerable road mileage, return the way you came.

Taking this northern section of railbed can add up to 4 additional miles to the tour, and is similar in nature to the south end.

Bicycle Repair Services

Accord Bicycle Service
Kerhonkson, NY
845-626-7214

Wheel and Heel
20 Route 17K, Newburgh, NY
845-562-1740

Information

New York State Department of Environmental Conservation, Region 3
21 South Putt Corners Road, New Paltz, NY 12561
845-256-3000

8
Ringwood State Park: Brushwood Loop

Location: *Ringwood State Park, Skylands section, Passaic County, Ringwood, New Jersey*
Terrain: *Hilly*
Distance: *6.5-mile sample loop; many other legal trails exist*
Surface conditions: *Variable-surface carriage roads with steep, rocky sections*
Maps: *Ringwood State Park (suggested); Trail Map 22: North Jersey Trails (New York–New Jersey Trail Conference) (recommended)*
Highlights: *State Botanical Gardens; miles of advanced off-road cycling terrain and beginner-appropriate carriageways; Shepherd Lake*

Ringwood State Park has become an increasingly popular destination for metropolitan New York mountain bikers. As of this writing, it represents one of the few extensive trail systems in proximity to New York City with enough mileage to keep avid cyclists interested; however, cyclists are being asked to avoid all singletracks at this time. Trail studies and unit management plans are developing for this park. The park service recently adopted a policy that certain trails will be designated for mountain bikers based on use patterns and trail sensitivity. While management personnel are in the process of finalizing these plans, cyclists are asked to use only the extensive carriage roads. It is anticipated that singletrack will become officially sanctioned when plans are finalized.

Management efforts, made in cooperation with cycling clubs and shops, have allowed for the development of a marked racing/training circuit in the near future. This will help contain cyclists in specific areas of the park; minimize impact and user conflicts, and secure the future of off-road biking in this resource.

Many people come to hike in the park, and the Shepherd Lake area—

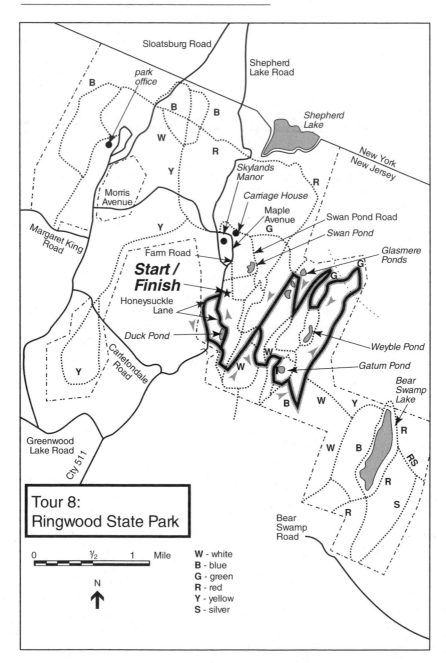

Sloatsburg Road

Shepherd Lake Road

park office

B

B

B

W

R

Y

Morris Avenue

Shepherd Lake

New York New Jersey

Skylands Manor

Carriage House

Maple Avenue

R

G

Swan Pond Road

Swan Pond

Glasmere Ponds

G

G

G

Margaret King Road

Y

Farm Road

Start / Finish

Honeysuckle Lane

Duck Pond

Carletondale Road

Y

W

W

W

Weyble Pond

Gatum Pond

Bear Swamp Lake

B

W

Y

R

Greenwood Lake Road

Cty 511

W

B

RS

R

Tour 8:
Ringwood State Park

S

Bear Swamp Road

R

| 0 | ½ | 1 | Mile |

W - white
B - blue
G - green
R - red
Y - yellow
S - silver

N

with its boat launch and rentals, bathing beach, and picnic area—attracts thousands of people annually. The park also allows hunting; be aware of season dates, and choose other tours during those periods. One of the largest attractions at Ringwood is the New Jersey State Botanical Garden at Skylands. This is the only botanical garden in the state park system and makes a worthwhile visit.

Ringwood Park can be reached from the NYS Thruway, NY 17, or NY 59 from the Sloatsburg area. It is also accessible from the west via County Route 91 (Skyline Drive northbound from Oakland) and Sloatsburg Road.

From Exit 15A on the NYS Thruway, go north on NY 17 (this is also NY 59 at this point) to a sign on your right reading RINGWOOD STATE PARK (2 miles if you were southbound on the NYS Thruway, 3.5 miles if you were northbound). Turn right; this is Sloatsburg Road. The park is 5 miles ahead (you're going to the Skylands section, which is beyond the main Ringwood entrance). Go 0.4 mile past the Ringwood State Park entrance, and turn left onto Morris Avenue, toward Shepherd Lake.

At 2 miles up Morris Avenue you'll reach the entrance booth. There's a small parking fee. Going to Shepherd Lake will cost you a few dollars more. If you don't plan to use the beach, it's more convenient to park at parking lot C, where the majority of mountain bikers park. You'll most likely be directed to that lot. (You can still ride your bike the short distance to Shepherd Lake and use the lake for no charge.)

After paying the entrance fee and getting your free Ringwood State Park map, turn right. The Carriage House—where there are phones and rest rooms—is to your left; Skylands Manor is on your right as you proceed along Maple Avenue, and the botanical gardens, where flowers are in bloom throughout the season, are to your left. At 0.2 mile bear right onto Farm Road, then bear left and pass parking lot B on your right. At the next intersection, bear left into parking lot C.

From parking lot C you can easily tour the botanical gardens in a large loop of just under 2 miles by following Swan Pond Road from the upper right-hand (northeast) corner of the lot. Bearing left on the white trail will take you past the Four Continents Statues on Crab Apple Vista, Swan Pond, the Wildflower and Bog Gardens, and the inner park, back to East Cottage Road and the Carriage House.

Whatever you choose to do, **carry a map.** You can get very lost in this park. Carry provisions, including first aid, water, and food. Use your

79

head and your map. Marking is poor. To begin the Brushwood loop, exit parking lot C.

0.00   At the intersection of lot C and two paved roads, go diagonally across the intersection, bearing left (don't go hard left, against one-way traffic) onto Honeysuckle Lane.

0.70   You'll see a right-hand turn onto a dirt road with a barrier gate. A sign reads MODEL PLANE FIELD. The dirt road splits. Go left, and climb easily.

1.40   At a four-way intersection go right on the (white) Crossover Trail.

1.45   Continue through an intersection.

1.60   At the top of a rise, with Gatum Pond to your right, turn right. Follow the earthen dam on the pond's west side. Go uphill, avoiding side trails.

1.80   At a poorly marked four-way intersection, continue on the (white) Crossover Trail.

1.90   A large open field to your right is the model plane field. You bear left.

1.95   The trail switches back hard to your right and goes uphill.

2.80   The trail levels off. The white trail heads southwest, but you go straight on the (blue) Pierson Ridge Trail.

2.90   Cross a gas pipeline.

3.10   Bypass the (green) Halifax Trail to your right and go around in a semicircle. Cross the pipeline again. Descend.

3.40   Turn right at a T.

3.45   Turn right at another T.

3.70   Go through a hairpin turn to join the (green) Halifax Trail.

4.20   Turn right at a switchback and four-way intersection. Descend.

4.70   Cross between the Glasmere Ponds, and turn left at the T.

5.80   Arrive back at the gate onto Honeysuckle Lane. Bear right. Ride straight, along a road flanked by large oak trees.

The entrance to Ringwood State Park (*photo by June Sanson-Kick*)

6.50 Turn right into parking lot C, or, if you parked elsewhere, return to the appropriate parking area.

Use your map to navigate the botanical gardens (staying on roads) or to visit Shepherd Lake.

Bicycle Repair Services

Campmor
18 Route 17 North, Paramus, NJ
201-445-5000

Barry's Bikes
5 Oakland Ave., Warwick, NY
845-987-1614

Town Cycle
1468 Union Valley Road, West Milford, NJ
973-728-8878

Information

Ringwood State Park
1304 Sloatsburg Road, Ringwood, NJ 07456
973-962-7031

9
Wawayanda State Park

Location: *Sussex County, New Jersey, Town of Highland Lakes, access from Warwick, NY*
Terrain: *Rocky and hilly*
Distance: *9.8 miles, optional 4-mile detour*
Surface conditions: *Dirt and gravel roads to rocky singletrack*
Maps: *Wawayanda State Park (available at park office); Trail Map 21: North Jersey Trails, Western Portion (New York–New Jersey Trail Conference)*
Highlights: *Single- and doubletrack riding on varied terrain suitable for intermediate and advanced riders; swimming beach; picnic area; many beginner trails*

A combination of singletrack, carriage road, swamp, rhododendron forest, and back roads, Wawayanda is one of the most attractive and biker-friendly state parks in New Jersey. With activities ranging from swimming in 255-acre Wawayanda Lake to picnicking, boating, fishing, group camping, and cycling, the 13,000-acre park is aptly described as an "oasis for nature and recreation" by the state's Division of Parks and Forestry.

The park has many more trails and through roads available to cyclists than are described in this tour. Several days of touring are possible without repetition. For instance, touring cyclists can ride some of the trails and the bike path between the park office and the lake that runs along Wawayanda Road. Note, however, that the outlying areas of Bearfort Mountain and Wawayanda Hemlock Ravine are not accessible to bikes because of their steep terrain, though both can be visited on foot. And whatever you do, stay off the Appalachian Trail.

A considerable black bear population inhabits the park, and you may

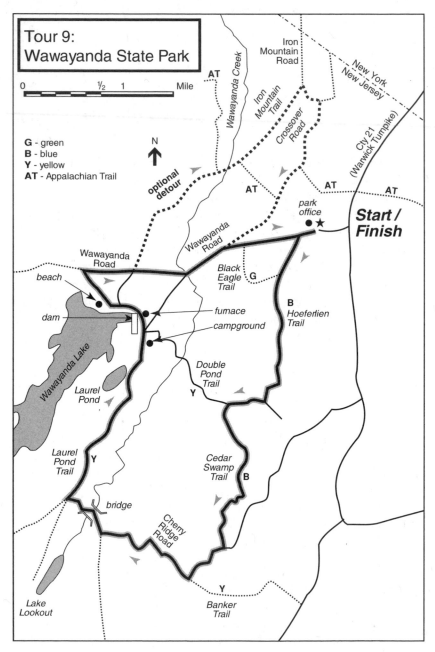

Tour 9:
Wawayanda State Park

0   ½   1   Mile

G - green
B - blue
Y - yellow
AT - Appalachian Trail

N

optional detour

Iron Mountain Road

Wawayanda Creek

Iron Mountain Trail

Crossover Road

New York
New Jersey

Cty 21 (Warwick Turnpike)

AT

AT

AT

AT

park office

Start /
Finish

Wawayanda Road

Wawayanda Road

beach

dam

fumace

campground

Black Eagle Trail

G

B

Hoeferlien Trail

Double Pond Trail

Y

Wawayanda Lake

Laurel Pond

Laurel Pond Trail

Y

Cedar Swamp Trail

B

bridge

Cherry Ridge Road

Lake Lookout

Banker Trail

Y

84

encounter a variety of wildlife. The park was at one time (1845–1890) the site of a mining village. Developed by the family of Oliver Ames, who built a blast furnace (which you'll see) and dammed the outlet of what is now Wawayanda Lake, the park contains this original 5600-acre Wawayanda Furnace property. A large section of the southwestern parklands—Bearfort Mountain—was originally the land of another ironmaster, Abram S. Hewitt of Ringwood fame. It appears that mountain bikers have benefited considerably from the country's early iron industry.

This tour lends itself to a day-long outing, which can culminate conveniently in a swim or picnic at the lake about 10 miles into the tour. You can ride the remaining few miles on either Wawayanda Road (a mellow, 35-mph road and bikeway) or through the woods on the Iron Mountain Trail. As of this writing, there is a small food concession at the lake, and there are facilities for cooking out.

The park is located in Highland Lakes, New Jersey, between West Milford, New Jersey, and Warwick, New York, on County Route 21 (the Warwick Turnpike). From the northern New Jersey area of Sussex, Morris, and Passaic Counties, you can reach Warwick via County Route 23 to County Route 94. From the north take I-84 to NY 17 east, and then head south on County Route 94. From Warwick, go 3 miles southwest on County Route 94 (toward New Milford), and turn left onto County Route 21. At 2.9 miles turn into the park entrance (on your right).

You can park outside the main office. There is no need to go through the toll and pay for lake-area parking. (If you arrive after 4 PM, entry to the entire area is free.) There are staff, maps, information, rest rooms, and a telephone at the office. There is no charge for biking as of this writing.

Find the trail a short distance from the office, about halfway between it and the tollhouses, on your left. Look carefully for the inconspicuous trailhead and sign reading WM. HOEFERLIEN TRAIL (blue).

0.00 *The trail starts by going uphill, then leveling out. It is rocky but easily negotiated. Marking is fair.*

0.50 *Reaching an intersection with the Black Eagle Trail (green on white), ride diagonally across, staying on the blue. Marking is good.*

The trail is rocky, rooty, and rarely level, but it's suited for intermediate riders.

1.80 At a T, turn right onto the Double Pond Trail (yellow). Marking is poor.

This area is low and very muddy after rain or in spring. Stay to the side.

2.20 Take the Cedar Swamp Trail on your left (blue, marked). Follow it, going slightly uphill.

2.30 Enter the cedar swamp and walk the plank boardwalks. You may have to carry your bike a short distance.

This is the habitat of the rare Atlantic white cedar and several endangered species.

2.60 Emerge from the swamp (if you've been careful, your feet are still dry).

2.70 At an opening in the forest, turn right (a vague footpath goes left—avoid it).

Follow the narrow, twisting, and sometimes rocky trail. Lift your bike over a few short, very rocky sections.

You'll be amazed at the solid wall of rhododendron surrounding you throughout much of the area.

3.50 Arrive at a T, the Banker Trail (yellow, poorly marked), and turn right onto a welcome doubletrack.

3.95 At a three-way intersection, turn right to join Cherry Ridge Road (dirt).

4.40 Cross a shallow creek where the road is washed out.

4.60 Cross an intact bridge over the Lake Lookout outlet, then watch carefully on your right for the Laurel Pond Trail (no marking).

4.80 Turn right onto Laurel Pond Trail, whose only cue is a tall, elegant stand of red pine trees (the bark is reddish brown). This is a singletrack, narrow but well defined, heading slightly uphill.

5.10 The trail, heavily marked in red, splits. Go left. This appears to be a re-marking from the original yellow.

5.40 The trail that split off at 5.1 (red) rejoins from the right.

A wilderness rest stop

5.80 Cross a small plank bridge.

5.90 At a T, turn left.

6.10 Cross a bridge over a small outlet creek from Wawayanda Lake. Climb easily.

6.60 Go through a barrier gate and into the camping area. Bear left.

6.65 At a five-way intersection you'll see the old iron furnace, a big stone structure, to your right. Go up the hill, leaving the furnace directly to your right.

6.75 Arrive at Wawayanda Lake. Bear right past a low dam to your left.

7.00 Pass through the boating area, continuing straight.

7.30 Arrive at the public beach and picnic area.

The lake is large and scenic—a nice place to rest.

As you leave the beach, follow Wawayanda Road. It's 2.5 miles back to the main entrance and your car.

If you wish, you can follow the Iron Mountain Trail (blue) back to the main gate in a route that will add 4 more miles to your trip.

Iron Mountain Detour

If you include this Iron Mountain Trail, your total trip distance is 12.7 miles.

0.00 Leave Wawayanda Lake beach area, turning right on Wawayanda Road.

0.60 Go left onto the Iron Mountain Trail (not marked; it is a wide doubletrack, or "jeep" trail. If you pass the GROUP CAMPING sign you've gone too far).

Continue on this trail. (There are many legal singletracks in this area.)

2.60 Bear right onto unmarked Crossover Road.

The Iron Mountain Trail bears left to leave the park, indicated by a small sign.

2.95 Bear right at a Y. (The left fork goes out of the park.)

4.60 Turn left on Wawayanda Road.

5.40 Arrive at the park entrance and your car.

Bicycle Repair Services

Campmor
18 Route 17 North, Paramus, NJ
201-445-5000

Dark Horse Cycles
2294 Route 208, Montgomery, NY
845-778-6604

Barry's Bikes
5 Oakland Ave., Warwick, NY
845-987-1614

Town Cycle
1468 Union Valley Road, West Milford, NJ
973-728-8878

Joe's Fix Its
20 West Main Street, Goshen, NY
845-294-7242

Information

Wawayanda State Park
885 Warwick Turnpike, Hewitt, NJ
973-853-4462

CENTRAL HUDSON VALLEY AND THE SHAWANGUNK RIDGE

The Shawangunk Ridge

Easily the single most popular spot for mountain biking in the Hudson Valley, the Shawangunks (pronounced "shongums"), or Gunks, are well-deserving of their reputation.

All of the ingredients for great mountain biking are here. Graded dirt roads and paths, a marked and maintained trail system, swimming and picnicking spots, incomparable scenery, and administrative units that are biker-friendly are just a few.

As the sport of mountain bicycling establishes its niche among the myriad forms of contemporary outdoor recreation, cyclists need to be aware of their natural setting as well as ways to minimize their impact upon it. What is now happening in the Gunks is a model of this that can be followed in other parts of the state or region—parts where cyclists may not be looked upon with cordiality by the better-known and stronger-lobbied groups, such as hikers and environmentalists, that have had to absorb another intrusion into their sanctuaries. As bikers treat a sanctuary, however, so shall they be treated, and to the credit of cyclists now using the Shawangunks, cyclists there are treated very well.

This is significant for several reasons. First, there are probably more environmental watchdog groups in the Gunks than anywhere within an equal radius of New York City, due to the extreme sensitivity and ecological significance of the ridge. You only have to spend a few moments in the place—even if you know nothing about it—to realize you are seeing someplace very special and unusual.

Second, the Gunks are getting more than their share of scrutiny these days, and issues of multiple use are often a subject of argument among the area's preservation groups. Anywhere else, this might put cyclists first on the chopping block; fortunately, though, a great many preservationists must be bikers.

The reason for this approach has a lot to do with the planned evolution of the ridge. The history of open-space planning in the area has been ambitious, and the attempt to define, regulate, and acquire lands considered integral to the system has been aggressive and successful.

Outside of the ridge, international organizations such as The Nature Conservancy have made known the ecological importance of this place. In 1993, the Conservancy identified 40 "Last Great Places" in an area including the United States, the Pacific Rim, and Latin America. The Shawangunks are among them. The identification and aggrandizement of these 40 great places has become the largest private fund-raising effort in conservation history.

This designation as globally significant habitat is due to the Gunks' dwarf pitch-pine community, which is the largest in the world, and to the profusion of rare and endangered species (about 60) living within the various ridge ecozones.

There is tremendous recreational and development pressure occurring within and around the ridge. Master plans for Minnewaska State Park have only recently been completed and are the subject of criticism by some groups. Organizations such as the Shawangunk Conservancy, the Open Space Institute, the Palisades Park Commission, the New York–New Jersey Trail Conference, Friends of the Shawangunks, and the Mohonk Preserve are working hard to balance these human needs against the interests of the environment, while at the same time accepting that humans are also a part of it. Think of them as you travel—they deserve your recognition and support. It seems amazing that with all they have to think about and protect, the cyclist has been maintained as part of the agenda.

In addition to the ridge's many interesting biological features, the area has a compelling history. From the early Huguenot patentees on the floodplain to the stone workers and commercial berry pickers of the high ridge, history is visible everywhere to the cyclist. These same carriage roads and scenic vistas have provided recreation for the past century. Whether they remain to accommodate the vast and growing numbers of recreationists of the next century depends on our behavior now.

Riding the Ridge—Minnewaska State Park

Bicycling rules at Minnewaska are adapted from IMBA (International Mountain Biking Association) rules and regulations. Riders must be very conscious of pedestrian/equestrian use. Bicycling is not permitted on hiking paths. Helmets are required, and regular policing is used to enforce the rule. Those in noncompliance are asked to leave.

Activities such as hunting, hiking, picnicking (fires in raised grills only), horseback riding, (cartop) boats, scuba diving, cross-country skiing, and swimming are encouraged. Permits are required for several of these. Because of the high level of public use of this park, other regulations are clearly stated and enforced: Glass containers, alcoholic beverages, and camping are not permitted. Parking is allowed only in designated areas.

For information contact Minnewaska State Forest Preserve (914-255-0752; fax 914-255-3505), PO Box 893, New Paltz, NY 12561. For after-hours assistance, contact New York State Park Police, 914-786-2781.

Riding the Ridge—Mohonk Preserve

To ride in Mohonk Preserve, you'll need to purchase either a preserve membership or a daily entry pass or be a guest at the Mohonk Mountain House. The preserve also asks that you adhere to its rules, which are designed to minimize user conflicts:

- Purchase a bicycle permit ($10, good from May 1 to April 30) and put it on your bike.
- Ride in single file and only on carriage roads.
- Maximum speed is 15 mph, or 5 mph when 30 feet from pedestrians.
- Dismount when 30 feet from carriages until they pass by.
- Alert pedestrians by bell or voice before passing them.
- Ride on the right.
- Give pedestrians and horses the right-of-way.
- Stop at a ranger's request and show your permits.
- Wear a helmet.
- Bikes are not allowed in the areas of Sky Top or the Mohonk House resort and lakeside.

Mohonk Preserve has a volunteer bike patrol. Its rangers also use bicycles. These people help to educate and manage other cyclists for everyone's benefit. Stop and talk with them if you have the chance. They are among the most knowledgeable park users and will be able to answer any questions you might have. For more information call Mohonk Preserve (914-255-0919), or Mohonk Mountain House (914-255-1000).

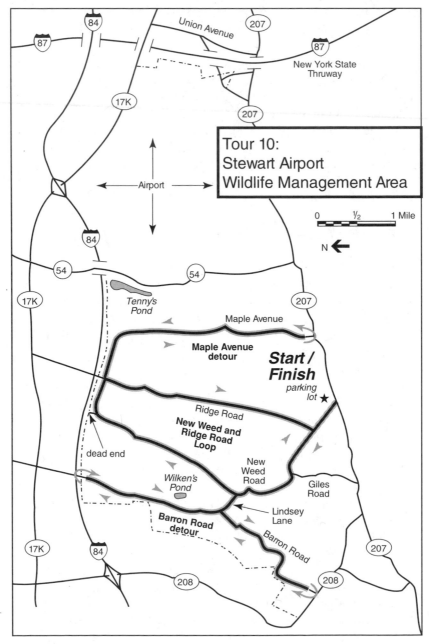

Tour 10:
Stewart Airport
Wildlife Management Area

Union Avenue

New York State
Thruway

Airport

0   ½   1 Mile

N ←

Tenny's
Pond

Maple Avenue

Maple Avenue
detour

Start /
Finish
parking
lot ★

Ridge Road

New Weed and
Ridge Road
Loop

dead end

Wilken's
Pond

New
Weed
Road

Giles
Road

Lindsey
Lane

Barron Road
detour

Barron Road

96

10
Stewart Airport Wildlife Management Area

Location: *Ulster County, Town of New Windsor*
Terrain: *Gently rolling*
Distance: *8-mile loop, 6.5- and 10-mile detours*
Surface conditions: *Broken pavement, gravel, dirt*
Map: *USGS Area Topographic Map, Walden; DEC map (see text)*
Highlights: *Dual-use trails that allow only hiking and bicycling; scenic and sequestered wildlife management area*

This unusual, scenic, private, and wild area gets little attention from bikers because it's not a state park, it isn't advertised, and it suffers from the connotations of its name. The reasons why few people might care to investigate cycling at an airport are understandable—few of us would dream of rides amid the overflight noise, concrete, and jet-fuel pollution associated with airports—and most are located in metropolitan areas, which mountain bikers are by definition trying to escape.

Stewart Airport is the exception. There are 6000 acres of land contained in the buffer zone, which was created in the 1970s. This state-owned property is primarily reclaimed farmland, some of which is still actively used.

Also, military installations lease space around the airport. The Army maintains helicopter- and hospital-evac units, an aviation unit, and an engineering office. Its main purpose is to house the overflow of soldiers from West Point. There is a Marine detachment as well as a division of the Air National Guard, which flies the tremendous C-5 cargo planes you'll see. But don't expect a lot of air traffic. The air guard flies only six or seven airlifts a week, over US and international space. The C-5s are more noticeable than regular commercial aircraft that fly from the airport because of their sheer size (the cargo deck on a C-5 can hold six Greyhound buses). These are the planes that recently supported Desert

Shield and Desert Storm and are the largest aircraft in the US inventory. They are also among the oldest (about 25 years) and loudest. Newer aircraft are quieter. But the C-5s will be around for another 40 or 50 years because they are too expensive to replace until needed.

As a result of public opposition to overflight noise, the air guard has obligingly located most of its training missions, with their constant take-offs and landings, in less populated areas of the country. Although there is steady commercial traffic, Stewart is not a busy airport like Kennedy, LaGuardia, or Newark. It was originally planned as a fourth jetport, however. When the Air Force left in 1969, during the Rockefeller era, development philosophies were more optimistic. Plans for Stewart included long runways into the existing buffer zone; there were even plans for a high-speed rail link from Manhattan. But a combination of factors, including the oil embargo and the creation of wide-bodied jets that could triple the capacity of existing aircraft, reduced the need and justification for another major jetport.

Today the buffer zone is quiet countryside with heavy populations of wildlife, particularly deer and wild turkeys. The area is managed by the New York State Department of Environmental Conservation. Cyclists must obtain Region 3 Cooperative Area access permits at the airport. They are free of charge. No cycling or hiking is allowed between September 30 and April 1 because of hunting season.

To reach the area from the New York State Thruway, get off at Exit 17 in Newburgh and follow signs for Stewart Airport. After leaving the tollbooths, bear left, setting your odometer to zero. Follow signs for NY 17K, turning right onto NY 17K (west) after 0.3 mile. At 0.5 mile turn left on NY 300 (Union Avenue). At 1.9 miles go right on NY 207 (west).

At 2.9 miles, turn into the Stewart Airport entrance to pick up your permit. Follow signs to the terminal. Take the first right after the terminal to 1038 First Street, four buildings past the terminal. Here a Department of Transportation representative will issue you the permit. Return to the airport's main entrance and turn right on NY 207, resetting your trip odometer.

At 3.8 miles—or a total of 6.8 miles from the Thruway ramp—park on your right where a sign says STEWART AIRPORT COOPERATIVE HUNTING AREA, STATE OF NEW YORK DEPARTMENT OF ENVIRONMENTAL CONSERVATION, REGION 3.

Begin here.

New Weed and Ridge Road Loop

0.00 Go through the steel gates, and start on New Weed Road.

0.20 Pass the DEC checkpoint. There are cornfields to your left.

0.50 At a four-way intersection, go straight. Ridge Road is to your right; the left-hand turn leaves the area.

1.20 Pass Giles Road to your left, which goes to NY 207.

By now you've noticed the variety of dirt trails and grassy side roads, but the airport's rules prohibit the use of these. Local bike clubs run racing circuits through these areas regularly.

Continue on New Weed Road.

1.90 At a Y, Lindsey Lane (dirt) goes left to join Barron Road. Go straight, staying on New Weed Road.

3.60 At a Y on a paved stretch, with I-84 ahead of you, bear right (the left is a dead end).

4.10 Turn right at a four-way intersection onto Ridge Road.

6.60 Pass apple orchards on the edge of a ridge. There are views of Mount Beacon and Dutchess County to the east.

7.20 At the same four-way intersection you passed at 0.50 mile, go left on New Weed Road.

7.70 Arrive back at the parking area.

Several detours and a great deal of casual riding are available at this area. To lengthen your ride, explore both Barron Road and Maple Avenue.

Barron Road Detour

0.00 Turn left off New Weed Road onto Lindsey Lane.

0.40 Go right on Barron Road.

0.90 Pass the old London Fog factory to your left.

1.00 On your right, a dirt side trail leads, after a short walk, to Wilken's Pond, an attractive rest stop. There are herons and beavers living here.

99

Views from Stewart Airport buffer zone (*photo by June-Sanson Kick*)

2.50 Barron Road ends, with I-84 to the north. Return to the intersection of Barron Road and Lindsey Lane.

4.60 Bear right, staying on Barron Road.

The trail here goes through more interesting and scenic countryside.

6.45 Arrive at NY 207 and return to Lindsey Lane.

Maple Avenue Detour

From the northernmost point of Ridge Road (the 4.1-mile point of the New Weed–Ridge Road Loop) go east, leaving Ridge Road to your right.

0.00 Begin on the paved road (motor vehicle use is illegal on all of the roads except during hunting season).

0.50 Pass a large wetland to your right at the northern extreme of Tenny's Pond.

0.75 Bear right onto Maple Avenue.

3.40 Upon reaching NY 207, you can return to your point of origin

or ride the road 1 mile west to your parking spot. If you choose the road, be extra cautious, as NY 207 is not safe for bicycles. It is preferable to return the way you came, then take Ridge Road back to the parking area.

7.20 Turn left on Ridge Road.

10.00 Arrive at the parking area on NY 207 and your car.

Bicycle Repair Services

Wheel and Heel
20 Route 17K, Newburgh, NY
845-562-1740

Joe Fix Its
20 West Main Street, Goshen, NY
845-294-7242

Information

New York State Department of Environmental Conservation, Region 3
21 South Putt Corners Road, New Paltz, NY 12561
914-255-5453

101

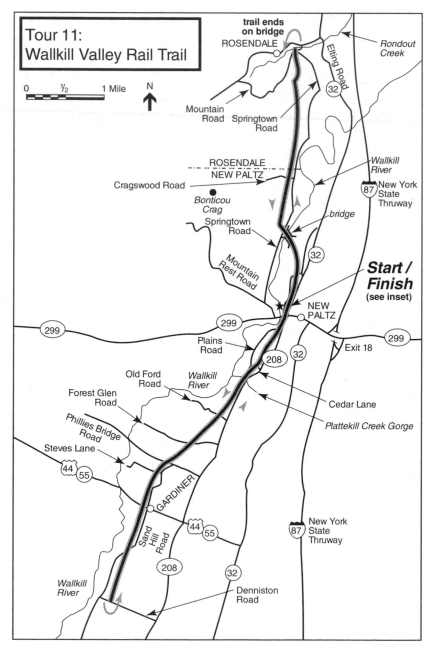

Tour 11:
Wallkill Valley Rail Trail

0   ½   1 Mile

N

trail ends
on bridge
ROSENDALE

Rondout
Creek

Elting Road

32

Mountain
Road

Springtown
Road

ROSENDALE
NEW PALTZ

Wallkill
River

Cragswood Road

Bonticou
Crag

87   New York
State
Thruway

bridge

Springtown
Road

32

Mountain
Rest Road

Start /
Finish
(see inset)

299

299

NEW
PALTZ

299

Plains
Road

Exit 18

208   32

Old Ford
Road

Wallkill
River

Forest Glen
Road

Cedar Lane

Plattekill Creek Gorge

Phillies Bridge
Road

Steves Lane

44   55

GARDINER

New York
State
Thruway

87

Sand Hill Road

44   55

208   32

Wallkill
River

Denniston
Road

102

11
Wallkill Valley Rail Trail

Location: Ulster County; towns of Rosendale, New Paltz, and Gardiner;
access from New Paltz
Terrain: Flat
Distance: Tour A, North: 13.2 miles; Tour B, South: 16.4 miles
Surface conditions: Gravel, dirt, cinder
Map: Wallkill Valley Rail Trail; USGS Area Topographic map, Rosendale
Highlights: Historic district (the oldest street in America in a continu-
ous state of habitation); views of the Shawangunk Ridge; state-of-the-
art linear park; rural atmosphere

The recent interest in greenbelt, heritage corridor, and linear park development has greatly benefited the cycling community in the Hudson
Valley. Although area trails have not been specifically designed for the
cycling public but rather for multiple-use applications such as jogging,
skiing, horseback riding, walking, and other forms of self-powered
recreation, it seems that cyclists use them most often. Rail trails in particular have been a blessing to bike riders, who, due to foot-trail overuse
and general exclusion policies, find it difficult to locate dirt tracks in
secluded countryside. Many older cyclists and those with families appreciate flat trails as well, because they are generally more accessible, well
maintained, and easier than the varied terrain of the uplands; yet they
offer distance, scenery, and, in many cases, a profusion of wildlife and
historic sites.

You can get a copy of the Wallkill Valley Rail Trail map in almost any
outdoor-related store in town. It isn't necessary to carry one to follow
the trail, but it's good to have, and if you want to be sure to have one
before starting the tour, write to the Wallkill Valley Rail Trail Association, PO Box 1048, New Paltz, NY 12561-1048. This is a private

group of volunteers who have worked hard to develop and maintain the trail. You might consider supporting them with your membership. The association prints a newsletter and holds annual events. Regulations and information have been placed at trailheads along the route on sign-boards, which also carry interpretive natural and historical information. The major complaints that the association receives from its various user groups concern the behavior and attitudes of bicyclists. Please be considerate, and alert pedestrians before you pass them. If you don't have a horn or a bell, just say hello.

The thick vegetation along much of the tour always brings with it a share of winged insects, so bring along a pair of glasses and some repellent if you're cycling in summer. You may want to bike this particular trail in the off-season when there are few bugs; the views are better, too.

This tour covers the northern and southern sections of the rail trail. If you have the time, do both; or save one for another day. But don't miss either of them. The southern section has excellent scenery, though it's not as established or as popular as the northern section, and its surface is not as consistent. The views of the Shawangunk Ridge, however, are much more sweeping and inclusive on the south end.

Naturally, you can begin at any place on the trail that you want, and there are several access points, but it is most convenient to leave and return from New Paltz, where you can get refreshments, information, and service for your bike. The villages of Gardiner at the south end and Rosendale at the north are the most extreme access points. Because of its proximity to the ridge and its many popular cycling areas, New Paltz has more than its share of bike shops. It is also a university (State University of New York) town, which adds to its color and vitality, and people from around the world come for the sole purpose of climbing the famous Trapps cliffs. You can watch them on the Overcliff/Undercliff Carriageway (see Tour 15).

Get off the NYS Thruway at Exit 18, New Paltz, and go left (west) on NY 299. Set your trip odometer, go through the village of New Paltz, and at 1.6 miles turn right onto Huguenot Street just before crossing the Wallkill River bridge. Head up Huguenot Street to a three-way intersection in the historic district, where a monument in the middle of the road commemorates the German Palatines who settled here. At this point turn right onto North Front Street and park. Go east a short way and you'll intersect with the rail trail.

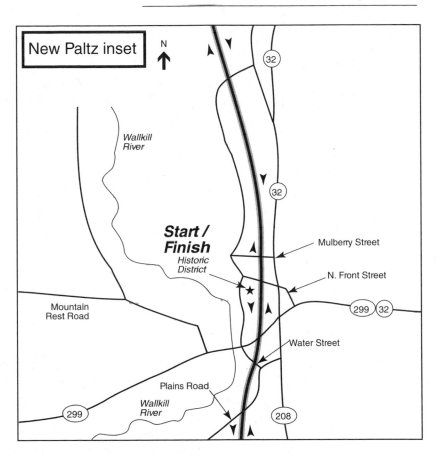

Tour A: Northern Section

0.00 *Leave North Front Street and travel north. The trail is a dou-*
bletrack gravel roadway at this point.

Within the first 0.5 mile you pass the historic district, and the old
stone houses of the original Huguenot patentees are well worth a
short side trip. It'll take you about 10 minutes to get off the trail
and ride up and down Huguenot Street, which you may elect to
do before you get on the trail. Broadhead Avenue is the location
of the Huguenot Historical Society, and Deyo Hall, the building

close to the west side of the rail trail, is the site of its museum. It's possible to tour the district and look inside some of the houses, which date back to the late 17th century (tours are scheduled).

A glass factory, lumber company, and cannery were located here, along with the community's first electric generating plant. Each was in proximity to the railway, which carried passengers as well as produce and equipment starting around 1866 under the name of the Wallkill Valley Railroad Company.

0.10 Cross Mulberry Street.

Interpretive signposts are placed at major road crossings along the rail trail, giving you natural and historic information. Take the time to read these signs as you travel, and look around at the forest cover and landscape to which they refer.

Although you are passing through a residential and commercial area of town, you begin to see bits of the ridge to the left, and a thin buffer of trees stands between the trail and the development on either side of you.

0.80 Cross Huguenot Street and continue north.

Diagonally across the street on your right is a large stand of juniper (red cedar) trees and, on a hill to your left, a group of mature white pines. You're heading for open country now, on a wide doubletrack with an excellent cinder surface.

In early summer you'll find a wide variety of wildflowers in bloom as well as a profusion of berries. Cherry trees are in bloom around Independence Day, and the byways smell sweet with cornfields, mulberry, sassafras, and sumac (not the poison kind, although there is poison ivy around).

1.70 Cross a small bridge in a backwater flat, with the main bridge over the Wallkill River just ahead.

1.80 You reach the river and bridge.

This bridge has been meticulously rebuilt and planked by volunteers, who finished in 1993. Their efforts on this project completed the section of trail between New Paltz and Rosendale. There are benches along the bridge, where you can sit and look over the copper-colored river, tinged by the runoff from agricultural lands.

As you continue on, the rock face to the north of you is Bonticou Crag. Located in the northern extreme of the Shawangunk Ridge on the Mohonk Preserve, it is a popular hiking destination that can be reached from the preserve trailheads off Mountain Rest Road.

1.90 *Cross Springtown Road onto a short section of singletrack.*

As you travel north, you'll pass through cornfields and private farms. Avoid straying onto the attractive-looking side trails in these areas; they are all private. With views of the ridge to your left, you enter a section of forest.

2.80 *Cross Cragswood Road, where the trail widens.*

3.50 *A signpost defines the town lines of New Paltz and Rosendale. The Rosendale section of the path is privately owned and is made available to the public courtesy of the owner.*

The terrain is ledgy and wooded through this stretch. Deer are common. At one point you'll cross an overpass and go through a short section of cutaway bedrock.

6.60 *Cross Mountain Road, and cycle onto the center span of the Rosendale Bridge.*

This is a spectacular spot, overlooking the village of Rosendale and Rondout Creek. The bridge is very high and commands caution. Youngsters should be closely supervised.

The rail trail ends here, blocked off in midspan. Discussion continues as to whether or not it will resume on the north side. You can reach the village by going left (downhill) on Mountain Road as you leave the bridge.

Touring cyclists use the rail trail regularly, and it's ideal for hybrid and cross bikes with almost any type of tire. Touring cyclists may return on a faster route by following Springtown Road, accessed from Elting Road, off Mountain Road. The fat-tire crowd, however, will be more content returning the way they came.

Tour B: Southern Section

To bike the south end you can also start from North Front Street.

0.00 *Begin, heading south.*

An original patentee home at the WVRT trailhead

0.10 *Cross NY 299.*

0.15 *Cross Water Street.*

Between here and Plains Road are several footpaths that lead to the river on your right. Views are better off-season.

0.30 *Cross Plains Road.*

From a parking area to the right of the trail as it crosses Plains Road, a short path leads to the river.

1.50 *Cross Cedar Lane. The trail widens.*

1.80 *Cross Plattekill Creek Gorge. There are excellent views of the ridge through this section.*

2.80 *Cross Old Ford Road.*

3.80 *Cross Forest Glen Road.*

4.60 *Cross Phillies Bridge Road.*

4.80 *Cross Steves Lane. You get a glimpse of the Shawangunks.*

5.60 Arrive in Gardiner. There are stores and a restaurant here. Continue south, immediately crossing US 44/NY 55 (Milton Turnpike), then Farmer's Turnpike, onto a singletrack.

6.70 Cross Sand Hill Road. Views are exceptional. The trail surface is excellent.

8.10 Reach the end of the trail at Denniston Road. From this point, you must return the way you came.

Bicycle Repair Services

The Bicycle Depot
15 Main Street, New Paltz, NY
845-255-3859

The Bicycle Rack
13 North Front Street, New Paltz, NY
845-255-1770

Table Rock Tours and Bicycles
292 Main Street, Rosendale, NY
845-658-7832

Accord Bicycle Service, Kerhonkson, NY
845-626-7214

Information

Wallkill Valley Rail Trail Association, Inc.
PO Box 1048, New Paltz, NY 12561

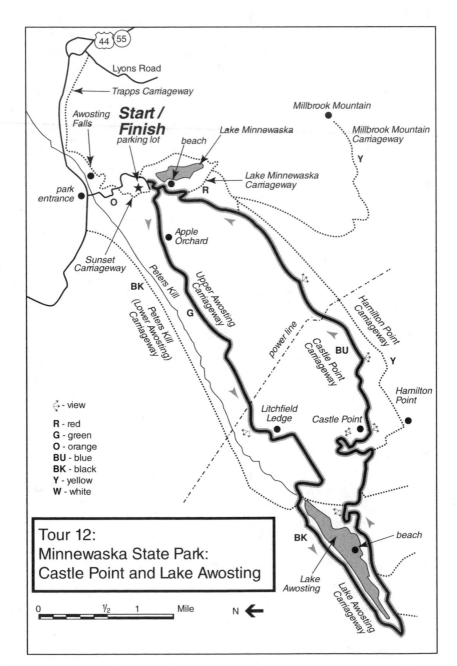

Start / Finish

44 55

Lyons Road

Trapps Carriageway

Awosting Falls

parking lot

beach

Lake Minnewaska

Millbrook Mountain

Millbrook Mountain Carriageway

Y

park entrance

O

R

Lake Minnewaska Carriageway

Sunset Carriageway

Apple Orchard

BK

Peters Kill

Peters Kill (Lower Awosting) Carriageway

G

Upper Awosting Carriageway

power line

Hamilton Point Carriageway

Castle Point Carriageway

BU

Y

Hamilton Point

Litchfield Ledge

Castle Point

⇕ - view

R - red
G - green
O - orange
BU - blue
BK - black
Y - yellow
W - white

beach

BK

Lake Awosting

Lake Awosting Carriageway

Tour 12:
Minnewaska State Park:
Castle Point and Lake Awosting

0   ½   1   Mile

N ←

12
Minnewaska State Park: Castle Point and Lake Awosting

Location: *Ulster County, Shawangunk Ridge; access from New Paltz*
Terrain: *Hilly*
Distance: *8 miles*
Surface conditions: *Graded and maintained gravel carriageways*
Maps: *Shawangunk Bicycle Routes (available at park entrance); Trail Map 9: Southern Shawangunk Trails (New York–New Jersey Trail Conference/Mohonk Preserve)*
Highlights: *Swimming at each end of the tour in Lakes Minnewaska and Awosting (in supervised areas only); outstanding scenic views of the Hudson Valley and the Catskill Mountains; marked, maintained, and patrolled trails*

Recent changes at Minnewaska State Park: Hamilton Point Carriageway has become a one-way route and may only be ridden in a north to south direction now. Adjust this ride accordingly.

Castle Point is one of the highest and most scenic destinations of the Shawangunk Ridge. At 2100 feet, it offers views that reach from north to southwest across the eastern Hudson Valley, and on the ascent from Battlement Terrace are some of the finest vistas of the Catskills to be found anywhere. The cycling here is beyond compare for scenic value, surface quality, variety of trails, and appeal to family, solo, or group riders.

Aside from the uncommonly rich setting, the main attractions of this tour are Lakes Minnewaska and Awosting, called "sky lakes" because of their high elevations. These can be appreciated whether you take advantage of the swimming or not. You'll be amazed by the deep viridian color and cleanliness of their waters, due to low nutrient levels and high acidity, which discourage plant and fish life. The relatively poor soil quality over the conglomerate rock comprising most of the ridge's surface is the cause of this nutrient deficiency. It is densely forested with pine, oak, and other poor-soil-related species, supporting rich and diverse populations of wildlife, some of which you'll see along the way.

The tour begins at Minnewaska State Park's main gate on US 44/NY 55, which is reached by taking the NYS Thruway to Exit 18, New Paltz, and going west on NY 299, toward the ridge that is the dominant visible feature of the landscape. Go through the village of New Paltz, crossing the Wallkill River at 1.6 miles. Continue until you reach US 44/NY 55 (where NY 299 ends) at 7.6 miles, where you turn right. Proceed uphill, soon passing by the vertical rock faces of the Trapps. The cars parked on the left (east) shoulder are typically those of climbers who come in great numbers to the rock along Mohonk Preserve's Undercliff Carriageway. Be alert for cyclists and pedestrians in this area.

Go under Trapps Bridge and continue heading west for another 3.2 miles to the entrance of Minnewaska State Park on your left. A modest entrance fee (adjusted seasonally) is required of those not in possession of an Empire Passport, a Golden Park Pass for seniors, or an access pass for the disabled (applications for these are available at the park office). Cycling maps and copies of the park rules and regulations are available here. Go uphill to the main parking area, at a higher elevation and north of Lake Minnewaska (which you'll see as you park). At the west end of the lot you'll find the trailhead, which is obvious and carries red markers at this point. There is a picnic area here, and fine views.

Go downhill, turning right at the fence above the lake, and continue a few hundred feet to the beach area, where you'll find signs and a posted map of the park's many carriageways. Portable comfort stations are placed seasonally at this location.

0.00 *Turn right onto the green Upper Awosting Carriageway.*

You'll see signs to Castle Point at the beach area, but don't follow them now. The grade is better on the Upper Awosting Carriageway, and you'll be coasting back on the steeper Castle Point Carriageway.

0.55 *Over undulating, easy terrain, you'll arrive at an opening in the forest referred to as the Apple Orchard.*

There are limited views to the west along this stretch of trail. If you arrive in mid-June, mountain laurel will be in bloom.

1.90 Pass under the power line.

2.30 Arrive at Litchfield Ledge.

This rock face has a northwest aspect and limited views. You'll travel in a wide arc around Huntington Ravine now, climbing moderately until reaching a T.

3.20 This is the intersection of Upper Awosting and Peters Kill (also called Lower Awosting) Carriageways. Turn right here and descend to the eastern edge of Lake Awosting.

There is a concrete dam here, and a good view of the lake. The small stream that leaves the lake is the Peters Kill.

3.50 Arrive at the black trail and go left (west). Pass the unoccupied ranger station on your right.

This section of trail around the lake is gullied and rockier in comparison to the park's major carriageways and is consequently less used. As you go west you'll be able to look back at the white cliffs of Battlement Terrace and Castle Point, your destination. You begin to get a feeling for the park's remoteness and size here, where foot trails amid stands of dwarf pitch pine depart for the Badlands.

As you ride around through the west and travel up the lake's eastern shore, you'll come upon a few isolated points. Watch for these on your left. If you want to explore the peninsulas, do so without your bike. These trails are herd paths initiated by hikers and can't stand up to the additional impact of bicycles.

5.50 Arrive at the Lake Awosting beach area.

This beach is actually a large, flat, rock slab with a sand and gravel bottom. Lifeguards are posted here in season; swimming while they are off duty is not permitted, and fines are imposed on violators. There is a Sani-Jon here.

6.00 Continuing on the black trail, you reach a viewpoint over the lake. A long, easy climb follows as you go toward Castle Point.

6.30 Turn right toward the Castle Point and Hamilton Point Carriageways.

6.80 Bear left toward Castle Point following blue markers. Stay ahead of children!

Relaxing on Castle Point, Minnewaska State Park

The trail climbs steeply here but can be pedaled with effort. Views in this area are excellent and increase in scope as you reach Battlement Terrace, the first series of ledges before Castle Point. Ride slowly and ahead of any children you have with you here, as the cliffs drop vertically and suddenly. To the north and west you'll enjoy an unusually wide panorama of the Catskill Mountains and lands south of the ridge.

7.50 *Arrive at Castle Point.* **Exercise extreme caution!**

There are no signs telling you where you are (and there's only an obscure one on Battlement Terrace), but you'll know you are someplace special when you arrive at this high, fissured precipice above the valley. The views reveal mountains and flatlands to the south and east that reach as far as the Hudson Highlands and West Point. In the foreground are Lake Awosting and the open parklands to the west. Below you to the east is Hamilton Point. It can't be reached by bicycle directly from Castle Point without backtracking to the previous intersection (see Tour 13). Also in view is a long ledge to the east, which goes to Millbrook Mountain and Gertrude's Nose. The conspicuous boulder on the ledge's northeast end is Patterson's Pellet.

Proceed downhill now for the rest of the trip, with only a few exceptions.

Be careful on some of the longer pitches where excessive speed should be avoided. Hikers and other cyclists will appreciate this, and you'll promote the (often challenged) notion that cyclists are safe and welcome additions to the park's many users. Remember to yield trail, and slow to walking speed while passing pedestrians.

Views of the valley and its many small hamlets continue to the east, and blueberries, which generally mature in midsummer, are especially profuse around here.

8.50 *Pass under the power line.*

9.50 *On your right, intersect with the trail that leads to Millbrook Mountain and the Hamilton Point Carriageways. Bear left toward Lake Minnewaska (1 mile).*

Continue following blue markers, going uphill to an open, grassy clearing with more views of the Catskills to your left.

10.00 Reach a T within sight of the lake. Go left, downhill, on the (red) Lake Minnewaska Carriageway.

10.50 Arrive at Lake Minnewaska Beach, your starting point. Go right, uphill, to the parking lot.

If you want an additional 2 miles of tour, mostly downhill, and have a driver who's willing to make the sacrifice, you can take the (orange) Sunset Carriageway down to Awosting Falls and proceed on the Trapps Carriageway to Lyons Road. It appears logical by the map to meet at benchmark 1242, where the trail meets US 44/NY 55, but it's illegal for cars to stop here, and rangers take these restrictions very seriously. Lyons Road is clearly shown on the conference map as well as the Shawangunk Bicycle Routes map at 1.5 miles east of the park entrance. Stopping (not parking) is permitted here.

Bicycle Repair Services

The Bicycle Depot
15 Main Street, New Paltz, NY
845-255-3859

The Bicycle Rack
13 North Front Street, New Paltz, NY
845-255-1770

Table Rock Tours and Bicycles
292 Main Street, Rosendale, NY
845-658-7832

Accord Bicycle Service,
Kerhonkson, NY
845-626-7214

Information

Palisades Interstate Park Commission (PIPC)
Bear Mountain, NY 10911-0427
914-786-2701; or 718-562-8688

13

Minnewaska State Park: Hamilton Point and Millbrook Mountain

Location: Ulster County, Shawangunk Ridge; access from New Paltz
Terrain: Hilly
Distance: 12.7 miles
Surface conditions: Graded and maintained gravel carriageways
Maps: Shawangunk Bicycle Routes (available at park entrance); Trail
  Map 9: Southern Shawangunk Trails (New York–New Jersey Trail
  Conference/Mohonk Preserve)
Highlights: Swimming (in season) in supervised areas of Lakes
  Minnewaska and Awosting; outstanding scenic views of the Hudson
  Valley and the Catskill Mountains

Recent changes at Minnewaska State Park: Hamilton Point Carriage-way has become a one-way route and may only be ridden in a north to south direction now. Adjust this ride accordingly.

Among the premier scenic destinations of the southern Shawangunks, Hamilton Point (2000 feet) and Millbrook Mountain (1500 feet) offer some of the best mountain biking in the East. These areas are accessible by wide, highly maintained carriageways—with a few exceptions. Certain locations along the trail are narrow and extremely dangerous. Inexperienced families with young or erratic riders should save this tour until capable levels of experience are attained, practicing instead on the preceding Castle Point and Lake Awosting tour (where caution is also required) or one of the other Minnewaska or Mohonk tours with minimal vertical drop exposure (see Tours 14 and 15). The difference with the Hamilton Point Carriageway is that you ride very close to the edge of cliffs at some points.

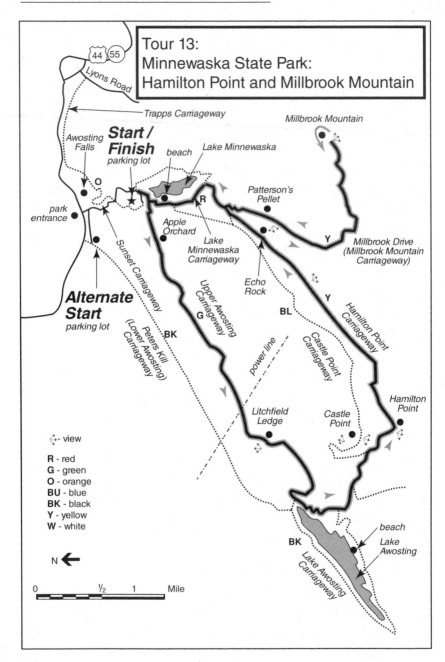

Tour 13:
Minnewaska State Park:
Hamilton Point and Millbrook Mountain

Trapps Carriageway

Millbrook Mountain

Awosting Falls

Start / Finish
parking lot

beach

Lake Minnewaska

O

R

Patterson's Pellet

park entrance

Apple Orchard

Lake Minnewaska Carriageway

BL

Y

Millbrook Drive
(Millbrook Mountain Carriageway)

Sunset Carriageway

Upper Awosting Carriageway

Echo Rock

Y

Hamilton Point Carriageway

Alternate Start
parking lot

Peters Kill
(Lower Awosting)
Carriageway

G

BK

power line

Castle Point Carriageway

Litchfield Ledge

Castle Point

Hamilton Point

beach

BK

Lake Awosting

Lake Awosting Carriageway

⟿ - view

R - red
G - green
O - orange
BU - blue
BK - black
Y - yellow
W - white

N ⟵

0   ½   1   Mile

The tour can be manipulated to meet your needs. Swimming is available at Lake Minnewaska, which you'll pass as you set out. You ride close enough to Lake Awosting to swim there, as well—with a 0.5-mile detour. Several adjoining carriageways (such as Lake Minnewaska or Lake Awosting) can be annexed to lengthen the trip, and there is enough legal bikeway to provide a series of excellent rides. Locals will tell you that they'll never tire of riding the Gunks. You, too, will find this area ideal.

There remains one admonition that riders will hear more of in the future: There is no singletracking in the park! Stay on the marked carriageways or we will all suffer. Be extra cautious around pedestrians, who may be pushing strollers. Give way to the many seniors who walk the ridge. Watch your speed and adhere to the IMBA rules printed on your map ("Shawangunk Bicycle Routes") and at the beginning of this book.

For this tour, get directions to Minnewaska State Park from Tour 12. Pay the fee and drive to the upper parking lot.

More aggressive cyclists should consider starting from the Peters Kill parking lot (enter at the main gate and turn right), to ride the carriageway by that name (also called Lower Awosting Carriageway) until it intersects with Upper Awosting Carriageway at the extreme east end of Lake Awosting. The Peters Kill Carriageway tends to see less use from pedestrians, except on busy days when the upper parking lot is full. It also provides an extra climb of about 500 feet to compensate for parking in the lower lot. The Peters Kill Carriageway, while very appealing, does lack the scenery of the Upper Awosting Carriageway. Don't let that discourage you, however—you'll get all the views you want from Hamilton Point and Millbrook Mountain.

Starting from the upper (main) parking lot, head out from its west end onto the trail. Ride downhill on the gravel path about 100 feet, to the fences overlooking Lake Minnewaska. There are picnic tables nearby. The area is scenic and open.

0.00 *Go right, downhill, on the red trail (Lake Minnewaska Carriageway).*

> *The swimming area is on your left. In season there are Sani-Jons here. Trail signs are posted.*

0.10 *Turn right onto the (green) Upper Awosting Carriageway. Although the Hamilton Point Carriageway may be shown as a left*

turn here on trail signs, stay on the Awosting, which will later join the Hamilton Point Carriageway. A gentle incline follows.

0.55 Pass an old orchard to your left. There are isolated views of the Catskills to your right at points along the trail.

2.00 Pass under the power line.

Slightly beyond this point you'll ride in a large semicircle beneath Litchfield Ledge and around Huntington Ravine. There are some views to the north. You begin to climb.

2.60 Reaching a T, go straight, following signs to Hamilton Point Carriageway (2.1 miles).

The righthand turn would take you to Lake Awosting's eastern shore, to a point where the Peters Kill Carriageway connects from the north. Riders coming up the Peters Kill (or Lower Awosting) Carriageway turn left at this point, keeping the lake to their right, to join the Lake Awosting Carriageway.

3.30 Arrive at an intersection where the black trail (Lake Awosting Carriageway) goes right. Continue straight.

3.90 At an intersection, go straight.

The right-hand (black) trail goes to Lake Awosting Beach, a 1-mile round-trip detour, where swimming is legal only when lifeguards are on duty.

Go easily uphill. There are views of Castle Point and Battlement Terrace along this 0.5-mile stretch.

4.40 At the T, go right, toward Hamilton Point.

You are now on Hamilton Point Carriageway (yellow). To your left is Castle Point.

4.75 Arrive at Hamilton Point.

Views here are excellent. Castle Point is above you and to the north; to the northwest and west is a large expanse of the park; to the east is an extended view of the Hudson Valley down to the Highlands and the ridges of Upper Westchester, Putnam, and the Taconics. *Be careful! There are dangerously high cliffs all along the point. Get off your bike before approaching the ledges!* Blueberry bushes are profuse, and berries may be ready by mid-July.

Leave Hamilton Point, continuing along the carriageway.

Hamilton Point

You'll travel downhill quickly through many curves and past more steep ledges. It is important for adults to ride ahead of children until reaching the vicinity of Echo Rock because the trail comes within several feet of vertical drops through this section. Keep your speed down. Watch for people on foot (and on bikes) ascending the carriageway.

Take a moment to enjoy the sprawling views to your right. (You'll be riding out onto the long ridge you see just ahead and to your right when you reach Millbrook Drive.)

7.30 *Turn right onto Millbrook Drive (also known as Millbrook Mountain Carriageway).*

The lefthand turn you passed just prior to this intersection is a short connector trail to the Castle Point Carriageway.

7.80 *The trail opens to a southwesterly view as you reach Patterson's Pellet. Continue along this undulating carriageway over an excellent surface.*

9.50 *Millbrook Mountain.*

Leave your bike at the bottom of the ridge and walk up the slab rock to an excellent view and resting spot. You are 1000 feet above the valley, looking north to south. Again, be cautious.

The vertical face below you, which can best be seen from the valley (or while driving up NY 299), is the one that world-class rock climber Fritz Wiessner spotted from farther south one day in 1935. He traveled north to climb it the next weekend, then explored Oberfall and Sky Top. The last area he climbed, the Trapps, is now the most popular. Millbrook became known as the "Old Route." A plaque commemorating Weissner and his partner, Hans Kraus, can be seen on the Undercliff Carriageway.

Return the way you came, to the Millbrook Drive intersection with Hamilton Point Carriageway.

11.70 *Turn right onto Hamilton Point Carriageway.*

12.00 *Turn left on the (red) Lake Minnewaska Carriageway. Stay on the red trail until reaching the swimming area and your starting point.*

12.60 *At Lake Minnewaska, turn right and go uphill.*

12.70 *Arrive at the parking lot and your car.*

If you are driving with someone else, one of you has the opportunity to coast downhill on Sunset Drive, get on Trapps Carriageway, pass Awosting Falls, and get picked up at Lyons Road. See Tour 12 for additional details.

Bicycle Repair Services

The Bicycle Depot
15 Main Street, New Paltz, NY
845-255-3859

The Bicycle Rack
13 North Front Street, New Paltz, NY
845-255-1770

Table Rock Tours and Bicycles
292 Main Street, Rosendale, NY
845-658-7832

Accord Bicycle Service,
Kerhonkson, NY
845-626-7214

Information

Palisades Interstate Park Commission (PIPC)
Bear Mountain, NY 10911
845-786-2701

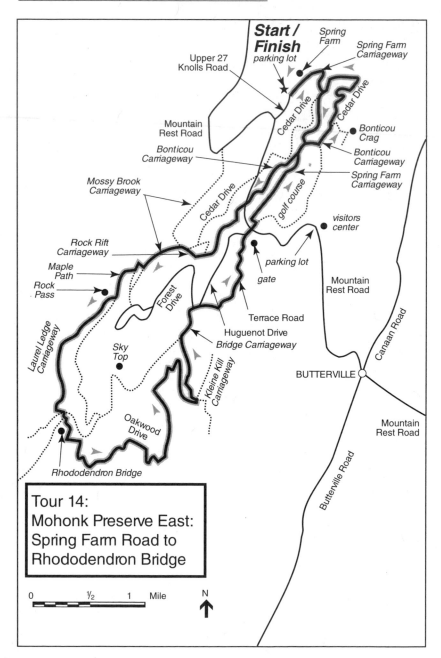

Start / Finish
parking lot

Spring Farm

Spring Farm Carriageway

Upper 27 Knolls Road

Cedar Drive

Cedar Drive

Mountain Rest Road

Bonticou Crag

Bonticou Carriageway

Bonticou Carriageway

Spring Farm Carriageway

Mossy Brook Carriageway

Cedar Drive

golf course

visitors center

Rock Rift Carriageway

Maple Path

Rock Pass

Forest Drive

parking lot

gate

Mountain Rest Road

Laurel Ledge Carriageway

Sky Top

Terrace Road

Huguenot Drive
Bridge Carriageway

Kleine Kill Carriageway

BUTTERVILLE

Canaan Road

Oakwood Drive

Mountain Rest Road

Rhododendron Bridge

**Tour 14:
Mohonk Preserve East:
Spring Farm Road to
Rhododendron Bridge**

Butterville Road

0   ½   1   Mile

N

14

Mohonk Preserve East: Spring Farm Road to Rhododendron Bridge

Location: Ulster County, Mohonk Preserve, Shawangunk Ridge; access from New Paltz
Terrain: Hilly with long, level stretches
Distance: 12.8 miles
Surface conditions: Shale-covered carriageways, 1 mile of paved road
Maps: Shawangunk Bicycle Routes (available at the Mohonk Preserve office or the gatehouse); Trail Map 10A: Shawangunk Trails, and 10: Shawangunk Trails North (New York–New Jersey Trail Conference/ Mohonk Preserve)
Highlights: Outstanding scenery; wooded carriage roads; minimal weekday use

This tour in the northern Shawangunks will introduce you to some of the most scenic and ridable country imaginable. The entire route is contained within the 6000-acre Mohonk Preserve, which has 22 miles of shale-surfaced carriage roads and an even greater distance of hiking trails. Trails are well marked and biker friendly. Mountain bikes may be ridden on carriage roads only and not in the vicinity of the resort hotel (Mohonk Mountain House). See "Riding the Ridge—Mohonk Preserve" in this section's introduction for information regarding day passes, bicycle permits, and membership. Although the area is heavily utilized (up to 100,000 visitors yearly), you'll see few people on weekdays.

After familiarizing yourself with the area on the two Mohonk tours in this guide, you'll be able to navigate most of the preserve using the specified maps and your own intuition. Traveling without a map here is not advisable. It's easy to get lost and wind up far away—on the side of this steep ridge *opposite* your car.

The Catskills from Spring Farm Carriageway (*photo by Larry Kosofsky*)

The tour begins with a steep but manageable incline; with the exception of a few short climbs, the remainder of it is level. Beginners in good condition should not hesitate to try it, but it may prove too long and challenging for younger children.

Take the NYS Thruway to Exit 18, New Paltz; turn left (west) on NY 299, and go through the village of New Paltz. At about 1.6 miles cross the Wallkill River and immediately turn right onto County Route 7, Springtown Road. Set your car's odometer. At 0.5 mile turn left onto County Route 6, Mountain Rest Road. At 1.8 miles go straight through the four-way intersection of Butterville Road, Canaan Road, and Mountain Rest Road. (This is Butterville.) Mountain Rest Road climbs steeply. At 3.4 miles the Mohonk Preserve visitors center is on your right. Stop here (park on the left) to get a bicycle permit and a day-use pass if you don't already have one. At 4 miles, pass the Lake Mohonk main gate and continue straight on Mountain Rest Road. At 5.1 miles, turn right onto Upper 27 Knolls Road. Go 0.2 mile to the end of the road, and park in the designated area.

0.00   Go through the steel gate. Get on Spring Farm Road and turn left, riding uphill.

The (blue) Table Rock Trail departs from here, directly across from the parking area. This is a foot trail only.

0.20 *Crest the top of a rise, where there is a sweeping view to the west of the Catskills and the lowlands, then descend.*

0.30 *Follow Spring Farm Road through a hairpin turn past Spring Farm (private).*

The trail then begins to ascend from an elevation of 690 feet.

0.50 *Reach a four-way intersection. Here, Spring Farm Road (also referred to as a carriageway) crosses Cedar Drive. Go straight, bearing left, on Spring Farm (don't bear right onto Cedar). You are heading west, climbing.*

1.00 *At the four-way intersection of Spring Farm and Bonticou Carriageway, go right onto Bonticou. At this point you're riding level at 1000 feet. Continue through this dense forest, recovering from the previous mile-long climb.*

1.80 *Cross Mountain Rest Road.*
Be careful here—cars will not expect you to suddenly appear from the woods. The drop from trail to road level is sudden and sharp. Pick up Bonticou Carriageway immediately on the other side of Mountain Rest Road.

You'll ride through a steep and wild hemlock ravine, which falls abruptly away to the north and climbs sharply to the left. The carriageway, however, remains level as it cuts its way around the headwaters of Mossy Brook.

2.60 *Bonticou Carriageway ends. Go straight, down Rock Rift Carriageway.*
At this intersection, North Lookout Carriageway goes left toward the Mountain House (no bikes!). A sign alerts the cyclist to the possibility of encountering equestrians.
Ride downhill. Watch your speed.

2.90 *Arrive at Cedar Drive and turn left.*

This section of "fairy-tale" forest has an ancient, ravaged, blown-down look about it. Large boulders covered in moss amid stands of hemlocks give you a feel for the northern Shawangunks.

3.00 *Turn left onto Mossy Brook Carriageway.*

Climb easily through this section of woods. Steep ledges to your left give way to sloping, open forest.

3.30   *Turn right onto Maple Path.*

       Mossy Brook Carriageway continues west, but bikes are not allowed beyond this point and must turn right.

       You'll see blue blazes and a narrow singletrack (which constitutes most of the legal singletrack in the entire preserve) on your right. Gear down and rock hop uphill. Recent changes in this trail may require some walking.

3.40   *Reaching the power line, dogleg about 100 feet to your left, and pick up the trail immediately to your right.*

3.70   *Crest a rise and descend.*

3.80   *Arrive at Laurel Ledge Carriageway. You must go right.*

At this intersection there is a large vertical rock face to your left and smaller ledges and crevices to your right, known as Rock Pass.

       Coasting, you get some views to your right of the Catskills.

       Passing by jumbles of boulders, you'll descend into a primordial-looking wetland area to your left, with ledges to your right.

5.10   *Arrive at Rhododendron Bridge and a four-way intersection. Cross the bridge, and turn right onto Oakwood Drive. This long, generally level carriageway of 3 miles takes you to the east side of the ridge.*

8.10   *At an intersection of several trails, go hard left onto Kleine Kill Carriageway (signs indicate which carriageway is which).*

       Ride uphill, passing a few isolated views of Sky Top (elevation 1542 feet) to your left (north).

8.60   *Forest Drive crosses the carriageway here, and Kleine Kill Carriageway becomes Bridge Carriageway at this point (no signs tell you about this transition). Continue straight.*

8.90   *Arrive at the (paved) intersection of Huguenot Drive and Terrace Road. Bear right, following Terrace Road (slightly uphill, then descending) toward the gatehouse. Since you'll share the road with cars, use caution. Fortunately this is only one-way traffic.*

10.00 Arrive at the gatehouse. Here you'll find a telephone, rest rooms, and a soda machine.

       From the entranceway to the gatehouse, on the west side,

cross the bridge, heading east, and turn immediately to your left onto Spring Farm Carriageway. (Don't go straight on Bonticou Carriageway toward the golf course—no bikes allowed.) Bear right, passing a few cottages.

10.40 Pass a trail on your right that goes to the golf course. Continue riding straight.

10.80 At the four-way intersection of Spring Farm and Bonticou Carriageway, bear right on Bonticou.

11.10 At this four-way intersection, go left onto Cedar Drive.

To your right the trail leads to the preserve visitors center. Hard to the left, going at a 45-degree angle into the woods, is the (red) Crag Trail, which is strictly a footpath.

This downhill section of Cedar Drive is rockier than the carriageways you covered earlier. Use caution.

12.30 Pass an old, broken-down stone foundation on your left; 100 feet beyond it, turn right onto Spring Farm Carriageway.

12.80 Arrive back at the parking area on Upper 27 Knolls Road.

Bicycle Repair Services

The Bicycle Depot
15 Main Street, New Paltz, NY
845-255-3859

The Bicycle Rack
13 North Front Street, New Paltz, NY
845-255-1770

Table Rock Tours and Bicycles
292 Main Street, Rosendale, NY
845-658-7832

Accord Bicycle Service,
Kerhonkson, NY
845-626-7214

Information

Mohonk Preserve, Inc.
PO Box 715, New Paltz, NY 12561-0715
845-255-0919

15

Mohonk Preserve West: Catskill Aqueduct to Trapps Bridge

Location: Ulster County, Mohonk Preserve, Shawangunk Ridge; access from New Paltz
Terrain: Hilly with long, level stretches
Distance: 16 miles
Surface conditions: Shale-covered carriageways
Maps: Shawangunk Bicycle Routes (available at the Mohonk Preserve office or the gatehouse); Trail Map 10: Shawangunk Trails North (New York–New Jersey Trail Conference/Mohonk Preserve)
Highlights: Outstanding scenery; wooded carriage roads

This tour will familiarize you with some of Mohonk's finest carriageways. It takes you from an elevation of 500 feet at the Catskill Aqueduct to just over 1000 feet on the Overcliff Carriageway. Most of the climbing takes place in a concentrated area, between Duck Pond and the intersection of Oakwood Drive and Kleine Kill Carriageway. The rest is a nearly level tour that takes in the incomparably scenic area known as the Trapps.

At the outset the terrain is steep—but never so steep that a cyclist in good condition will have to walk. The rest of the tour can be treated as "recovery." This tour can be managed by strong beginners and families.

To start the tour, follow the directions from the NYS Thruway (Exit 18) given in Tour 14, resetting your odometer at the Butterville Road–Canaan Road–Mountain Rest Road intersection (Butterville). From this four-way intersection, continue straight on Mountain Rest Road for another 0.5 mile until you see an unmarked gravel parking area on your right. On the opposite side of the road is the continuation of the Catskill Aqueduct (it also goes east from where you are parked).

If you don't have a day pass or a bicycle permit, keep going on Mountain Rest Road another 0.8 mile until you reach the Mohonk Preserve offices and visitors center on your right, where you can purchase them. If the office is closed, you can purchase passes from one of several rangers who patrol the area, especially around the Trapps. Remember, these funds are needed, and you are helping to preserve a spectacular ecosystem.

0.00 *Begin, crossing Mountain Rest Road and riding west along the aqueduct.*

The Catskill Aqueduct transports water underground to New York City. You are riding along the top of the berm. This right-of-way is not always maintained, and grass may grow high along here. Ride in the established ruts. There are dense woods on both sides of you. This section of trail is flat.

1.20 *Cross a dirt road (Lenape Lane).*

1.40 *Watching carefully, turn right onto a narrow trail marked in blue. You'll see Mohonk Preserve signs here. Stay on this trail, crossing a creek.*

1.70 *Go right, uphill.*

1.90 *Arrive at Duck Pond.*

There are views of Sky Top to the left.

You'll begin to climb after you pass the pond. Stay on Duck Pond Road, avoiding side trails or singletracks. (This road is sometimes referred to as Kleine Kill Carriageway.)

2.40 *As you pass through an area of open fields, there are views to your left of Sky Top, and to your right is a large expanse of the Hudson Valley. Continue riding straight. (Avoid the right turn at mile 2.6.)*

2.80 *Turn left onto Oakwood Drive at the four-way intersection of Oakwood and Kleine Kill Road. This section is flat.*

4.20 *Travel through an open field on a wide turn. The rocky, rough trail to your left (Glory Hill) leads back to Duck Pond. Go straight, staying on Oakwood Drive, which takes you along the edge of the east-facing Shawangunk Ridge across several ravines.*

5.60 *Arrive at Rhododendron Bridge. Note the map embedded in*

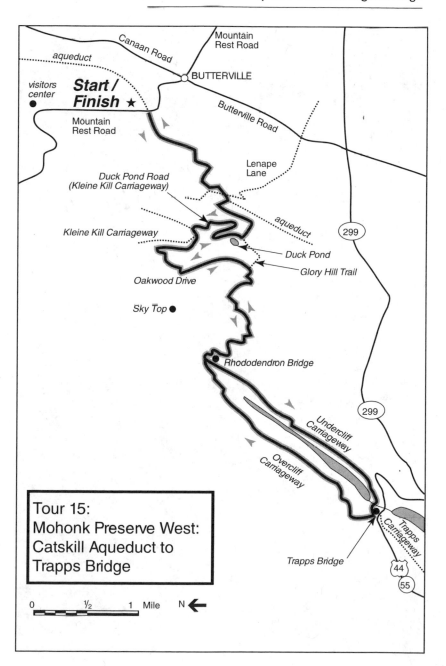

Canaan Road

Mountain
Rest Road

aqueduct

BUTTERVILLE

visitors
center
●

**Start /
Finish** ★

Butterville Road

Mountain
Rest Road

Lenape
Lane

Duck Pond Road
(Kleine Kill Carriageway)

aqueduct

(299)

Kleine Kill Carriageway

Duck Pond

Glory Hill Trail

Oakwood Drive

Sky Top ●

Rhododendron Bridge

(299)

Undercliff
Carriageway

Overcliff
Carriageway

Tour 15:
Mohonk Preserve West:
Catskill Aqueduct to
Trapps Bridge

Trapps
Carriageway

Trapps Bridge

(44)

(55)

0   ½   1   Mile   N ←

133

The Trapps, Undercliff Carriageway

stone on your right. Bear left onto Undercliff Carriageway.

The next 5 miles comprises a loop through a sensitive area, heavily used by various groups. Especially on weekends, you'll need to control your speed and watch for pedestrians.

7.60 *Stop to read the climbing history posted at the climber's kiosk.*

You'll see climbers all through this area and hear their echoes among the cliffs. Before leaf-out you'll be able to get a good look at these high vertical rock faces and watch climbers close up on the next few hundred feet of wall that reach down to the carriageway.

The atmosphere is quiet so that climbers on the rock faces can talk to their anchor partners on the ground. Since they usually have their gear on the carriageway and are often anchored nearby, slow down or, preferably, walk this stretch. A piped spring exists here just west of the kiosk. Nobody will vouch for its purity, but many do drink from it.

This is a fascinating spot. Idle climbers are often interested in talking about their sport and will encourage you to get involved. After seeing some of the easier climbs as you approach Trapps Bridge, you may find yourself thinking it over. You can get a safe, enjoyable introduction to the sport by engaging one of the many guides who teach in the area. Check the kiosk or inquire at the preserve office.

Continue going straight.

8.00 *Arrive at the three-way intersection of Trapps, Overcliff, and Undercliff Carriageways at Trapps Bridge.*

The bridge is just to your left, but don't cross it. There are Sani-Jons here. Often a ranger is posted at either the bridge or the climbing area (on weekends); he or she will be helpful and informative.

Amid the huge rubble stones and scree of the Trapps, bear right onto Overcliff Carriageway. This is the halfway point of the tour.

Overcliff Carriageway provides some of the best Catskill Mountain views available anywhere. Long slabs of white conglomerate make good resting and viewing posts along the way. This is a popular trail. Watch for joggers, pedestrians, and oncoming cyclists, especially at the blind turns.

From the open ridge with westerly views, descend into a deep forest and control your speed.

10.50 Cross Rhododendron Bridge and turn right onto Oakwood Drive, retracing your steps to Duck Pond.

13.50 Arrive at the four-way intersection of Kleine Kill and Oakwood Drive. Bear right, downhill.

14.60 Turn left onto the aqueduct.

16.00 Arrive back at your car.

If you've got the energy and interest in doing another (flat) 3 miles, you can continue on the other (east) side of the aqueduct— a scenic, easy tour that dead-ends 1.5 miles to the north.

Bicycle Repair Services

The Bicycle Depot
15 Main Street, New Paltz, NY
845-255-3859

The Bicycle Rack
13 North Front Street, New Paltz, NY
845-255-1770

Table Rock Tours and Bicycles
292 Main Street, Rosendale, NY
845-658-7832

Accord Bicycle Service,
Kerhonkson, NY
845-626-7214

Information

Mohonk Preserve
PO Box 715, New Paltz, NY 12561-0715
845-255-0919

16
Hurley Rail Trail

Location: *Ulster County*
Terrain: *Flat to gently rolling*
Distance: *17 miles round-trip*
Surface conditions: *Cinder, dirt, grass, and broken rock*
Maps: *Ulster County; USGS Area Topographic Map, Kingston East*
Highlights: *Forest cycling; wetlands; historic High Falls; Delaware and Hudson Canal and museum; Rondout Creek*

The Hurley Rail Trail is unexpectedly attractive and ridable. It is maintained and managed by a local group of cyclists, working in cooperation with the Delaware and Hudson Canal Heritage Corridor Alliance, who are currently signing and marking the trail and expanding it in both directions. As of this writing, there are no maps available, but don't let that stop you—the trail is self-guiding and in very good condition over its entire length.

The trail has a noteworthy history in terms of its organization and development, which began with a grassroots-style effort and wound up being funded by several sources, the most recent being a matching grant of $50,000 from the Environmental Quality Bond Act Fund, part of a $6.7 million EQBA funding package for park and recreation projects in 20 counties across the state. This grant will provide for construction of an extension of the trail through Marbletown, the land being donated to the town by Ulster County. The money will be used to grade the trail, clear it of debris, and make it suitable for cyclists and joggers. Motorized vehicles of any kind are prohibited, but access points for emergency and maintenance vehicles will be provided. While the local highway department will be involved in the work, it is to be compensated by money from the grant. As a result, taxpayers won't pay for any part of the pro-

137

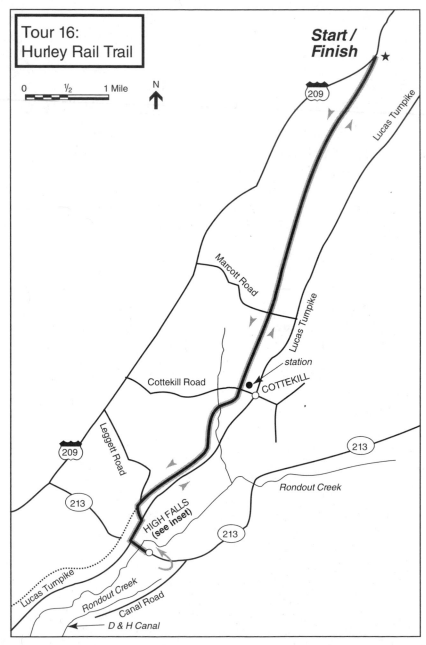

Tour 16:
Hurley Rail Trail

0   ½   1 Mile

N

Start /
Finish

209

Lucas Turnpike

Marcott Road

Lucas Turnpike

station

Cottekill Road

COTTEKILL

Leggett Road

209

213

213

Rondout Creek

213

HIGH FALLS
(see inset)

Lucas Turnpike

Rondout Creek

Canal Road

D & H Canal

138

ject. But even though non–trail using taxpayers may be happy to avoid footing the bill for such things as trail development, a "heritage corridor"—support for which is rising in several New England states—will directly benefit a wide cross-section of any community because of the concurrent increase in recreational, educational, preservational, and economic development.

The D&H Heritage Corridor connects several features of regional historical significance within the 35 miles between the Catskill Mountains and Shawangunk Ridge. The Hudson Valley has been a leader in this type of economic and recreational development. To quote Congressman Maurice Hinchey, "The endeavor to revitalize the D&H Canal is providing a national model for citizen participation in establishing scenic corridors and greenways." Readers who are interested in mobilizing their own communities can start by contacting the D&H Canal Heritage Corridor Alliance, c/o The D&H Canal Museum, PO Box 23, High Falls, NY 12440. Ask for their "Handbook for Action."

For this tour, get off the NYS Thruway at Exit 19, Kingston. Turn right (west) onto NY 28, following signs to US 209. Go south on US 209, and in about 3 miles you'll see the trail sign on your left. Pull off at the trailhead, and park on the side of US 209. The trail is blocked by a cable here. Plans are being made for a parking area.

0.00 *Begin by going around the cable and heading south through the woods.*

2.50 *Follow a long, narrow wetland.*

Wildflowers are profuse here. Watch for deer and waterfowl as well as songbirds nesting in the tangles of standing dead trees and blowdowns. In the summer months you'll see the typical loosestrife, goldenrods, and lady's thumb, but be on the lookout also for the less common, water-loving cardinal flower.

3.40 *Cross Marcott Road and continue straight.*

The trail narrows from a "carriageway" width to a wide singletrack. You'll pass through a hemlock ravine and dense hardwood forests.

4.00 *Cross a small stream. Approach with caution. The bridge is out but is scheduled for replacement.*

4.40 *Cross Cottekill Road near the old rail station.*

Site of former aqueduct in High Falls, New York

The station is now a private residence. The trail singletracks at this point, and although it starts out rough, it soon returns to an excellent surface. The character becomes more rugged than before as you cycle past farm fields and through stands of pine.

4.70 *You reach a shallow ravine where a trestle collapsed. Follow the trail around to your left and climb the south side to continue.*

6.30 *The trail ends here, at Leggett Road. Although it appears to continue just across the road, this section is not completed. Turn left here and left again on Lucas Turnpike, which you'll reach within 0.25 mile. At the bottom of the hill, ride left into High Falls village on NY 213.*

7.50 *Arrive in High Falls.*

Keep going until you see the DePuy Canal House restaurant on your right. Just beyond its eastern wall is a grassy spot, good for lunching, and a large, beautifully preserved section of the D&H Canal. A bronze plaque embedded in its wall reads THIS SITE POSSESSES EXCEPTIONAL VALUE IN COMMEMORATING OR ILLUSTRATING THE HISTORY OF THE UNITED STATES. The canal is a narrow, deep construction of stone block that at one time held enough water to float barges full of cement, coal, and passengers from Pennsylvania to New York City. It operated from 1828 to 1898, running alongside the Delaware River and Rondout Creek to Eddyville, with a total length of 108 miles.

You can ride this section of the canal and come back to the village in about a mile-long detour, or you can lock your bike and walk the path. There was a towpath on each side of the trench at one time, and you can still see the wear marks that were worn into the stone by the tow ropes.

7.60 *Leave the canal house and follow the trail immediately to the right of the canal itself, which leaves from the rear of the restaurant. Go slightly uphill over a trail that's not officially maintained but is in good condition. Watch for pedestrians, and keep children away from the canal's edge.*

8.00 *Reaching DePew Road, you may either return on the canal trail, or follow the road to the left and go left again on Canal*

Road. This will bring you to Mountain Rest Road (also called Mohonk Road). Go left, into the village.

To your right just before reaching High Falls is the D&H Canal Museum, a worthwhile place to visit if you have the time.

8.40 *Turn left onto NY 213 to return to the rail trail.*

9.00 *To your right just before the bridge are the High Falls Historic Park and hydroelectric generating facility.*

This area is worth a stop. It's on the river, there's a picnic table overlooking the falls, and if you care to wheel your bike through the gate, you can glide down along the river for a look at the old aqueduct site, where the stonework and steel rods of a suspension bridge carried the canal across the creek. This structure was built by John A. Roebling, who later built the Brooklyn Bridge. The aqueduct was suspended on cables that were 8 inches thick. This is a scenic, secluded, peaceful section of water.

9.70 *Leave High Falls village.*

10.10 *Turn right onto Lucas Avenue.*

10.40 *Go left onto Leggett Road.*

10.70 *Pick up the rail trail on your right.*

12.00 *Reach the ravine, and push your way up the other side.*

12.60 *Go straight across Cottekill Road.*

13.70 *Cross a paved road.*

16.90 *Arrive back at the trailhead and your car.*

Bicycle Repair Services

Accord Bicycle Service
Kerhonkson, NY
845-626-7214

Bike Brothers
139 Boices Lane, Kingston, NY
845-336-5581

Kingston Cyclery
1094 Morton Blvd., Kingston, NY
845-382-2453

Big Wheel
1774 Ulster Ave., Lake Katrine, NY
845-382-2444

Overlook Mountain Bikes
93 Tinker Street, Woodstock, NY
845-679-2122

Information

D&H Canal Heritage Corridor Alliance
c/o The D&H Canal Museum
PO Box 23, High Falls, NY 12440; or
PO Box 176, Rosendale, NY 12472-0176

143

CATSKILL FOREST PRESERVE

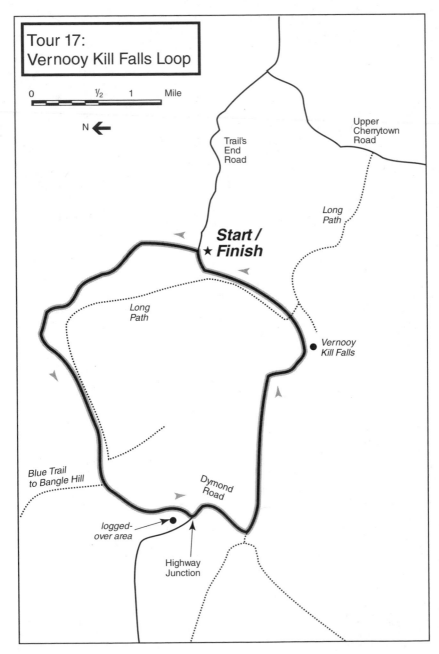

Tour 17:
Vernooy Kill Falls Loop

0   ½   1   Mile

N ←

Trail's
End
Road

Upper
Cherrytown
Road

Long
Path

Start /
★ **Finish**

Long
Path

Vernooy
Kill Falls

Blue Trail
to Bangle Hill

Dymond
Road

logged-
over area

Highway
Junction

146

17
Vernooy Kill Falls Loop

Location: Ulster County, Town of Rochester, Sundown Wild Forest
Terrain: Slightly hilly forest roads, snowmobile trail
Distance: 14.6 miles
Surface conditions: Dirt roads and singletrack, rocks, ruts, mud
Maps: Ulster County; USGS Area Topographic Maps, Kerhonkson, West Shokan, Peekamoose Mountain, Rondout Reservoir
Highlights: Vernooy Kill Falls

This is a deep-woods ride that will take you into a large section of the southeastern Catskill Forest Preserve. It's an excellent choice for riders who have "missed the gate" at Mohonk or Minnewaska—having arrived after those parking lots are full—and it stands on its own as an area where a very different form of biking can be enjoyed. Aggressive bicyclists who are unfamiliar with or feel restricted by the protocol at Mohonk and Minnewaska will enjoy Vernooy Kill much more—and will make everybody on the ridge happier for their decision. The area is also suited for campers, novice riders, and sturdy families out to try some serious mountain biking. It is not an area recommended for very young children, beginners, or those unfamiliar with wilderness use.

An outlying, off-road, multiple-use area, Vernooy Kill Falls has much more to offer the mountain biker than just the loop itself. Several trails, both single- and doubletrack, depart from the main route, and by following the tour directions given here, you'll pass most of them. Some of these will terminate far from your return destination, so be extra cautious to avoid getting lost. This is not a small state park or defined area like that encompassed by many of the other tours in this book, but a 27,000-acre stretch of forest with no signage off the suggested route. **Carry first-aid supplies and tire repair tools!** And bring insect repellent.

147

Ryan Kick contemplating a swim at Vernooy Kill Falls

All of these trails are legally open to cyclists as of this writing. The New York State Department of Environmental Conservation must be given credit for including mountain biking in its unit management plans for Sundown Wild Forest. No user conflicts have been reported so far, and to prevent this from happening in the future, I discourage you from using sections of biking thoroughfare that, while legal, are traversed by the Long Path. The tour has been routed accordingly.

For this tour, take the New York State Thruway to Exit 18, New Paltz, go west (left) on NY 299 and through the village, downhill toward the Wallkill River (about 1.5 miles). As you cross the Wallkill River bridge and see the Shawangunk Ridge in front of you (you'll drive over it) set your odometer to zero. Go straight. Be careful not to bear right on the west side of the Wallkill, toward Mohonk. Stay on NY 299 until it ends at a T at 6 miles, and turn right onto US 44/NY 55. Climb steeply through a hairpin turn, leaving the high cliffs (the Trapps) to your right, passing under Trapps Bridge at 7.5 miles. Pass the Minnewaska State Park entrance on your left at 10.7 miles.

At 17 miles and another T, turn right onto NY 209. Reset your trip odometer to zero here, especially if you've been coming north on NY 209 from another area. At 1.5 miles north on NY 209, turn left onto Ulster County 3 (Pataukunk Road). At 3.4 miles from NY 209, go left onto Lower Cherrytown Road. Watch carefully. After 1.2 miles bear right onto Upper Cherrytown Road (if you see Baker Road, you've gone too far).

Watch for blue paint marks along the road here—the traditional Long Path blazes. After 3 miles you'll see the hikers' and snowmobilers' parking lot on your right (the trail enters the woods on the left), but don't park here. You are free to ride on this section of trail, but I don't recommend it: It goes uphill, it's gullied and prone to erosion in some areas, and it will carry the largest population of hikers in the area. A much better place to begin lies ahead, at the top of Trail's End Road.

Keep going past the parking area, and at 1.2 miles go left. A little over a mile on Trail's End Road, which turns to dirt, will bring you to a primitive area where camping is permitted. You may not be able to reach the lot without a four-wheel-drive or a high-ground-clearance vehicle, but road conditions may have improved. Try it. If you can't make it, simply park along the road, keeping far to the right, and bike up to the trailhead.

At this point you'll find trail signs, snowmobile markers, and blue trail markers.

149

0.00 Go right on a doubletrack woods road, following the sign that reads HIGHWAY JUNCTION; GREENVILLE VIA NORTH LOOP.

This section of trail is a town road that is sometimes used by four-wheel-drive vehicles.

0.40 Singletracks will appear here and there.

The area is heavily forested with oak and laurel. The road is pot-holed and can be wet. Ruts are minimal. You'll travel slightly up-hill.

1.20 A doubletrack trail intersects the road here with signs advising CLOSED TO MOTOR VEHICLES.

This area is open for exploration if you are experienced in navigating through wilderness areas.

1.40 Cross a bridge over a small creek.

There is a ridable trail to your right here, heading east.

1.75 Washouts may occur through this area. Mud can be a problem.

1.90 Cross a wooden bridge with a campsite to your left.

Camping in "established" sites in New York State Forest Preserves is legal, and normally signs are posted to indicate legal areas. However, state law does not allow camping within 150 feet of any stream or trail, or outside of an established (previously impacted, legal) area. Rangers do patrol this area.

2.50 Pass a cabin (private) on your right.

The trail is rocky here, but conditions improve.

2.60 Pass a dirt road to your left that descends slightly.

2.90 The blue trail goes right toward Bangle Hill and ultimately to the Peekamoose Valley. This is part of the Long Path that cyclists are asked to avoid.

3.40 Enter a logged-over area.

3.70 Arrive at "Highway Junction."

You'll see signs reading SOUTH LOOP, VERNOOY KILL FALLS TRAIL 0.5 M. Turn left, following paved Dymond Road.

4.20 Turn left into the woods again, where signs read SOUTH LOOP TO FALLS 2.0, and CHERRYTOWN ROAD 3.8.

This is a rocky, rooty trail closed to motor vehicles (except snowmobiles). It looks like a difficult surface at first, and it is more technical than the previous doubletrack, but it's an excellent trail, mostly singletrack. Watch for snowmobile markers. The soil here is primarily peat and duff. Use caution. There are large, sharp rocks and thick roots.

5.00 *Enter a forest of dwarf hemlock. After a brief uphill, the trail begins a long downhill.*

6.20 *Arrive at Vernooy Kill Falls.*

This is the place for a break and lunch. The "falls" is a series of cascades falling a total of about 60 feet. There are several large, clear pools. Swimming is at your own risk; there is no supervision. Of course, after lunch, remember to carry out what you've carried in.

Downstream of the bridge is a ruined wall of the Vernooy Mill complex (1700s–1809).

Having crossed the bridge, three trails are visible. Pass the first, sharp-left trail (unmarked and close to the creek), and take the middle, left-bearing trail. Don't follow signs to Upper Cherrytown Road since this will lead you to the hikers' parking lot (1.8 miles).

Follow this westernmost trail slightly uphill over a cobblestone surface. This section of multiple-use trail is a piece of the Long Path. It is so rocky you'll make little impact. Watch for hikers in this area, and give them plenty of space.

7.20 *Pass the Long Path cutoff on your left.*

7.33 *Arrive at the starting point on Trail's End Road.*

You'll agree, by now, that this is an attractive area and a valuable resource to multiple-users, especially mountain bikers, who currently have the lowest allotment of designated trail miles in the Catskill Forest Preserve. We should be thankful, as the preserve's newest user group, to have any—and in the Sundown Wild Forest there are plans to develop more. For information, write to the New York State Department of Environmental Conservation at the address below.

Bicycle Repair Services

Accord Bicycle Service
Kerhonkson, NY
845-626-7214

Bike Brothers
139 Boices Lane, Kingston, NY
845-336-5581

Kingston Cyclery
1094 Morton Blvd., Kingston, NY
845-382-2453

Big Wheel
1774 Ulster Ave., Lake Katrine, NY
845-382-2444

Overlook Mountain Bikes
93 Tinker Street, Woodstock, NY
845-679-2122

Information

New York State Department of Environmental Conservation, Region 3
21 South Putt Corners Road, New Paltz, NY 12561
845-256-3000

18
Harding Road

Location: *Greene County, Town of Palenville, Catskill Forest Preserve*
Terrain: *Extremely hilly and mountainous; 2000-foot climb*
Distance: *12.7 miles (more available if desired)*
Surface conditions: *Roughly half pavement (uphill on NY 23A), half dirt and washed-out doubletrack; some steep and rocky stretches*
Map: *Trail Map #41: Northeast Catskills (New York–New Jersey Trail Conference); Greene County; USGS Area Topographic Map, Kaaterskill*
Highlights: *North Lake State Campground; swimming holes; spectacular scenery; historic location*

This historic route, which is now a horse and foot trail ascending the largest, deepest clove in the Catskills, is as rigorous as it is amazing. The views are far-reaching, the scenery is up close and—in the clove—savage and wild, and the grades are steep. **It is suited for advanced, self-sufficient riders only!**

We owe the existence of this particular road, running from the valley level to escarpment top (a vertical rise of 2000 feet), to a piece of chicken! As it turns out, the escarpment area around North Lake was so attractive to early hotel builders that one, namely Erastus Beach, placed his Catskill Mountain House on the cliff's edge in Pine Orchard in 1823. The emerging leisure classes of New York and Philadelphia, spurred by the transcendentalist movement and their newfound wealth, migrated to the big hotel for the next century or more. When a star boarder, millionaire-lawyer George Harding, asked that his daughter Emily be served fried chicken instead of the standard fare (her diet allowed no red meat), Mr. Beach refused. "Go and build your own hotel" is what he ungratefully told Harding. And so Harding did . . . on the next hill south

153

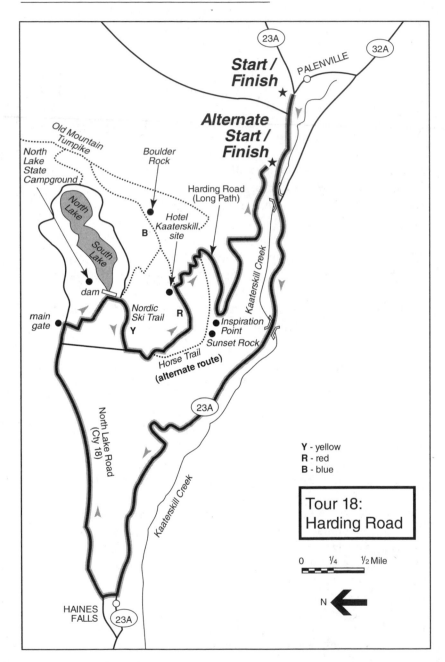

Tour 18: Harding Road

Y - yellow
R - red
B - blue

0   ¼   ½ Mile

N

of Beach's Catskill Mountain House. Emily named it the Hotel Kaaterskill. It opened for business in 1881, but there was the problem of access. Harding couldn't use Mr. Beach's Mountain Turnpike (see Tour 18), for obvious reasons, so he decided to build his own. After being told by railroad engineers that the project would be expensive and impractical, a few local men were hired, and the road was built by hand and steam power. You can read accounts of the remarkable "Fried Chicken War" in Alf Evers's *The Catskills: From Wilderness to Woodstock* (Overlook Press), or in *Kaaterskill: From the Catskill Mountain House to the Hudson River School,* produced by the Mountain Top Historical Society.

There are several ways of opening this tour. I strongly recommend that you initially visit North Lake State Campground, which could act as a starting point. This is a first-class, well-maintained facility with all the ingredients for great family camping: boating, boat rentals, fishing, swimming in cold, spring-fed waters, lakeside or wilderness camping, picnic sites, and miles of scenic hiking trails. Regardless of the fact that the Harding Road and the other escarpment tour in this guide, the Old Mountain Turnpike, are rigorous and demanding tours, the campsite itself and surrounding dirt paths provide—where permitted—excellent family cycling opportunities for touring or off-road bikers.

A group could camp, swim, picnic, and bike throughout the campsite and upper escarpment area, while the better riders among them could ride the trail down to Palenville, to be retrieved later. A two-car pool could leave one car in Palenville (at the bottom) and one at the top, shuttling to avoid pedaling the considerable uphill. Or, a pair of strong riders could park in Palenville, ride up, and return to their car after the downhill leg. Assuming you choose the latter course, you have the choice of biking up either Harding Road or Route 23A. The road is less frustrating, and traffic, though heavy on weekends, is slower than most. The scenery is worth the effort, and there's an excellent swimming hole on the way. This is a serious workout!

For this tour, get off the NYS Thruway at Exit 20 in Saugerties. Follow NY 32 north (toward Hunter) onto NY 32A and into the town of Palenville (about 8 miles); turn left onto NY 23A. Set your trip odometer. Watch very carefully to your right (north) after passing through Palenville, and at 0.6 mile you'll see a very small, undeveloped parking spot just before the CATSKILL PARK sign. The area trailhead is marked by a state land designation sign and horse-trail markers. Parking is limited

155

here—there's room for only two cars. It will probably be necessary for you to park in town and bike the half mile or so to the trail. The Harding Road trail leaves from this small parking lot. However, the first half of this tour, as described, is on the highway. Be extremely cautious of traffic.

If you want to use two cars, leave one at the Harding Road trailhead (or nearby if the lot is full) and the other at the North Lake Campground (follow the directions below).

0.00 *Assuming you have to start from the village, set your bicycle's odometer at the intersection of NY 23A and NY 32A in Palenville. Head north on NY 23A (toward Hunter).*

0.60 *Pass Harding Road (also the Long Path and horse trail) on your right.*

0.90 *Cross a bridge over Kaaterskill Creek.*

1.50 *Cross the creek again.*

There are excellent swimming holes just under this bridge. You can carry your bike over the guardrail to keep it in view. Swimming here is at your own risk. Continue uphill.

5.00 *Turn right onto North Lake Road in Haines Falls (Greene County Route 18). You'll see a sign for North Lake at this intersection. Continue to climb gently for another 2.2 miles.*

7.30 *Reaching the North Lake State Campground, pass through the main gate and turn immediately right. To ensure accuracy, and for those starting the tour at North Lake, reset your bicycle's odometer to 0.0.*

0.00 *Go through the main gate and turn immediately right, riding downhill to the lake.*

0.55 *Cross an earthen dam at the south end of South Lake, and begin to go uphill slightly.*

0.60 *Look carefully to your right, and take the yellow-marked Nordic Ski Trail. This is a rocky but very ridable doubletrack. You can cruise at 10 mph.*

1.00 *Arrive at a four-way intersection. A series of signs will greet you. Don't follow the sign marked TO SOUTH MOUNTAIN TRAILS. Go left, uphill.*

June at the ATB Trail, North Lake State Campsite

> *Follow red markers toward Sunset Rock, Inspiration Point, and Boulder Rock (none of which is your destination). You'll also see a sign for Sleepy Hollow Horse Trail (which you are on). Follow the horse trail uphill over rock. Water bars have been placed in the trail.*

1.50 *Reach an intersection where the horse trail departs to your right. Go straight, on the red trail, toward the Kaaterskill Mountain House site (1.3 miles), Boulder Rock (2.2), and North Lake Campground (2.9).*

2.30 *This is the highest elevation you'll attain (2400 feet) and the site of the now-demolished Hotel Kaaterskill (also called a "mountain house"). A short loop trail encircles the hotel site. This three-way intersection has several signs.*

To the east on the blue trail is Boulder Rock. This is a good trail for exploring, but it turns rocky. Boulder Rock is not legally accessible by bike.

Turn right here, going downhill.

2.70 *Reaching a T, go left. Signs here will say* HALFWAY HOUSE LOOKOUT 1.2, RIP VAN WINKLE HOLLOW REST AREA 3.4, *etc.* Harding Road *(which you are on) is not indicated. You're back on the horse trail now.*

2.90 *(This horsetrail can be used as an alternate, flat detour. If you take it, you'll miss the hotel site, avoid a great deal of uphill, and arrive at milepoint 2.7) Turn right. There's a trail to your left, and signs reading* HALFWAY HOUSE LOOKOUT *and* RIP VAN WINKLE HOLLOW. *See Tour 18, Old Mountain Turnpike, for descriptions of these areas.*

The trail heads steadily and steeply downhill here; control your speed. There are ledges to your right and a steep drop to your left. **Use caution!** Younger riders should stay behind the more experienced. There are views of the clove to your right as you switchback and head east.

4.00 *Cross a deep ravine and hemlock-forested gulch with a seasonal tributary of the Kaaterskill running through it.*

4.10 You'll reach a hitching post and lookout area, where you can see down to NY 23A and up into Kaaterskill Clove. Continue downhill over loose rocks and broken bedrock.

4.80 Pass a road to your left. This doubletrack is not posted. It leads to an area with a private hunting camp. Go straight.

5.40 Descend the last section of Harding Road and into Palenville, to your car.

Bicycle Repair Services

Philthy O's
6000 Main Street, Tannersville, NY
518-589-0600

Information

New York State Department of Environmental Conservation
1150 North Westcott Road, Schenectady, NY 12306
518-357-2234

159

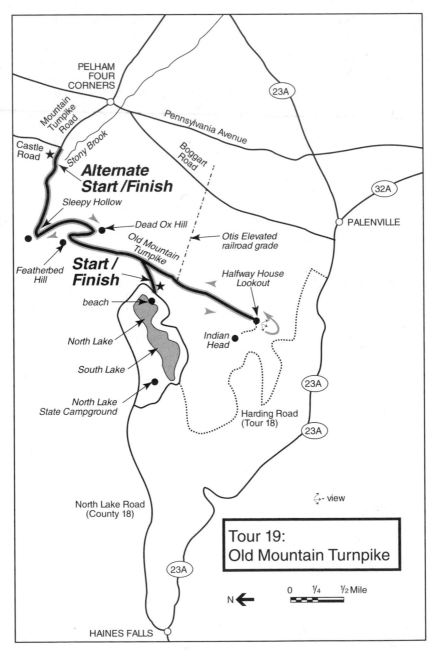

PELHAM
FOUR
CORNERS

23A

Mountain Turnpike Road

Pennsylvania Avenue

Stony Brook

Castle
Road

Boggart Road

**Alternate
Start /Finish**

Sleepy Hollow

←Dead Ox Hill

*Old Mountain
Turnpike*

32A

PALENVILLE

←— Otis Elevated
railroad grade

*Featherbed
Hill*

**Start /
Finish**

*Halfway House
Lookout*

beach —

North Lake

*Indian
Head*

South Lake

*North Lake
State Campground*

*Harding Road
(Tour 18)*

23A

23A

⟷- view

*North Lake Road
(County 18)*

Tour 19:
Old Mountain Turnpike

0   ¼   ½ Mile

N ←

23A

HAINES FALLS

19
Old Mountain Turnpike

Location: Greene County, Town of Palenville, Catskill Forest Preserve
Terrain: Extremely hilly and mountainous; 2000-foot climb
Distance: 16 miles (7 of them dirt/rock)
Surface conditions: Roughly half pavement (uphill on NY 23A), half dirt and washed-out doubletrack
Maps: Map #41: Northeast Catskills (New York–New Jersey Trail Conference); USGS Area Topographic Map, Kaaterskill
Highlights: North Lake State Campground; swimming holes; spectacular scenery; historic location; highly challenging

Just the name "Old Mountain Turnpike" sounds magical enough to attract backwoods explorers, rock hoppers, and the inveterate bush bikers among us, but it only hints at the romantic history of the place.

Washington Irving—America's first prose stylist and the man credited with developing a distinctive national literature—never actually visited the Catskills before penning "Rip Van Winkle," the story that brought them world renown. He only saw them from a river steamer! It is likely he knew of Kaaterskill Falls, however, and the large amphitheater beneath the first tier, where some say Rip slept away the better part of a lifetime. By 1819, when Irving wrote the story, this amphitheater had long been a popular landmark with Native American guides, Revolutionaries, hunter-trappers, and, at last, surveyors, and was "the best piece of work" James Fenimore Cooper's Hawkeye had ever seen in the woods (*The Pioneers*, 1823). It was not Irving, however, who placed Rip Van Winkle on the map, but hotel purveyors, the first tourist admen of new America.

Along with capitalizing on myth in an effort to bring wealthy New York guests to the hotel he built in 1823, Erastus Beach had more practical considerations. He had to build a road. It was to bring visitors in ox-drawn wagons from their berths on river steamers to the misty edges of Hawkeye's "all creation." The road was quite an accomplishment for its time, climbing 2000 feet from the valley floor to the perch of Pine Orchard's—and America's—first real "mountain house." Those early teamsters named a section of it "Dead Ox Hill," hinting at its character. Indeed, a climb up this road was as grand as a stay in the hotel itself. And, according to hotel literature and employees, it was on this very road—the Old Mountain Turnpike—a stout walk from Kaaterskill Falls at a turn beyond Black Snake Creek, that Rip Van Winkle lived.

Today it represents one of the few trails to penetrate the escarpment from the valley. Harding Road, a few miles to the south (see Tour 18), is another. Old Mountain Turnpike descends steeply from North Lake State Campground in Haines Falls in several long "levels," which switchback radically at several points. It ranges in surface from smooth dirt to bedrock, cobble, and clay-gravel, but most of it is rocky. It must be considered only by advanced riders, fully equipped with first-aid and bike maintenance supplies. It is not recommended for families or casual riders. Like Harding Road, this route is for the very capable mountain biker.

There are four ways to approach the trailhead. If you can arrange a ride, start from North Lake and get picked up in Palenville. This way you avoid the strenuous climb. If you like strenuous climbs, however, you can park at the bottom of the trail, ride up, and then return. If you prefer to ride up on pavement, you can take the scenic route up Kaaterskill Clove to North Lake. An even more challenging outing can be had by climbing Harding Road and descending Old Mountain Turnpike in a loop that involves only a short section of road. Assuming that most solo or one-car riders will prefer to do the steep uphill ride on pavement and save the best part—the downhill—for last, the tour directions here begin at the bottom of Old Mountain Turnpike.

See Tour 18, Harding Road, for driving directions to Palenville. Just beyond the only traffic light in town, heading north on NY 23A (toward Haines Falls and Hunter), look for Boggart Road on your right. Follow it for 2.5 miles until you reach Mountain Turnpike Road on your left. This is Pelham Four Corners. There's a small dirt road to your right. Following signs to the Sleepy Hollow Horse Trail (synonymous with the Old Mountain Turnpike), turn left, drive 0.8 mile to the dead end, and park on your right, to the side of the road. The trail is just ahead of you.

Pine Orchard, location of the view of James Fenimore Cooper's "All Creation"

To bike the roads up to North Lake, as I recommend, go back to NY 23A and turn right, setting your odometer. At 5 miles, turn right onto County Route 18. Go 2.2 miles farther to the campsite entrance. From this point, continue straight on the campsite road to the end, at North Lake Beach (1.5 miles).

Find the top of Old Mountain Turnpike due east of the beach bath-house. Don't make the mistake of going down the Otis Elevated railbed, which is farther south and to your left. The turnpike actually starts from the picnic area and is marked with snowmobile and horse-trail disks. Walk your bike east, heading toward the valley with your back to the bathhouse, and within 100 yards you're on the trail.

0.00 Head downhill.

0.60 There's a trail to your right here. Follow it as it leaves the turnpike and goes downhill, turning south (you'll be returning to the turnpike later).

1.00 Cross the Otis Elevated railbed, a wide scar running in a straight line down the mountain.

Opened in 1892, the railroad (a cable-driven, gravity-incline arrangement) was a quicker, more comfortable alternative to the turnpike.

Enter the woods again on a narrow trail. Go straight.

1.70 Ignore a fork to your left just prior to this set of trail signs to Halfway House Lookout (your destination).

2.35 Arrive at Halfway House Lookout.

At 2100 feet over the valley, there are excellent views here of Kaaterskill High Peak, Roundtop, and a large section of Kaaterskill Clove and the valley.

Another very interesting overlook—Indian Head or Point of Rocks—can be reached by following an unmarked footpath west. Halfway House Lookout is a popular resting place for equestrian groups and overnight campers. Beware of vertical drops.

Return to Old Mountain Turnpike the way you came.

3.80 Go right, downhill, on the turnpike.

This section of the road was known historically as the Long Level. Much of its upper end is grassy, but it soon turns rocky.

5.00 Switchback on Featherbed Hill, staying on the turnpike. This section is known as the Short Level.

5.25 Switchback onto Dead Ox Hill. There's a crude campsite and rest area here at a site known as Cape Horn, elevation 1600 feet. Proceed downhill.

5.90 You reach Sleepy Hollow, also known as Rip Van Winkle Hollow.

Here are the scant remains of an early "halfway house," where coach travelers could rest. Later, it became the "home" of Rip Van Winkle himself. Rip's Boulder (where he slept) and Rip's Rock (600 feet above you on a trail system accessible only from Winter Clove) are nearby landmarks.

Proceed downhill, crossing Black Snake Bridge. Several old trails appear beyond here, with a few prominent ones leading

north onto private lands. Isolated water holes (shallow in summer) exist in Stony Brook, to the right of the trail.·

7.00 *Finish on the pavement where you are parked or have arranged to be picked up.*

Those who have chosen not to climb Old Mountain Turnpike can now see the merit of their choice. If you wish to make a loop of this trail by joining it to Harding Road, follow the directions for Tour 18. Upon reaching the cutoff trail to Halfway House Lookout and Rip Van Winkle Hollow near the top of Harding Road (2.5 miles uphill from NY 23A), turn right, heading downhill. The lookouts are visible from that point, directly to the east and downhill.

Bicycle Repair Services

Philthy O's
6000 Main Street, Tannersville, NY
518-589-0600

Information

New York State Department of Environmental Conservation
1150 North Westcott Road, Schenectady, NY 12306
518-357-2234

UPPER HUDSON VALLEY

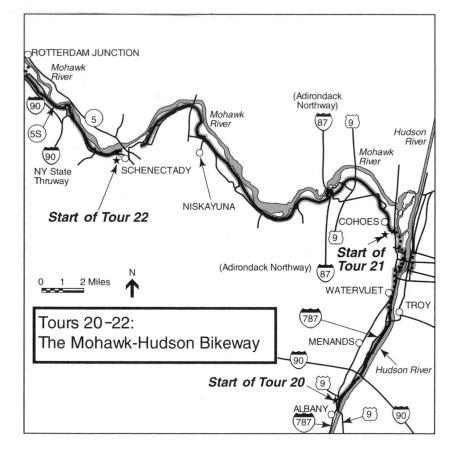

ROTTERDAM JUNCTION

Mohawk River

(Adirondack Northway)

90

5

5S

87   9

90

Hudson River

Mohawk River

NY State Thruway

SCHENECTADY

Start of Tour 22

Mohawk River

NISKAYUNA

COHOES

9

Start of Tour 21

0   1   2 Miles

N

(Adirondack Northway)

87

WATERVLIET

TROY

Tours 20–22:
The Mohawk-Hudson Bikeway

787

MENANDS

90

Hudson River

Start of Tour 20   9

ALBANY

787

9   90

168

The Mohawk-Hudson Bikeway

The Mohawk-Hudson Bikeway is a winding, flat, very scenic trail located along these two historic rivers. Regarded by the New York State Department of Transportation as "one of the region's most notable and popular recreational features," the bikeway (like so many linear, multi-municipality parks) is a cooperative project among New York State and the counties and towns it connects.

This is a trail for the avid commuter, jogger, walker, and recreational or athletic cyclist wishing to exercise on a regular basis between mountain tours. It's highly recommended for beginners, families, and cyclists at any ability level and is widely used by these recreational groups. The trail can be cycled in the three separate tours described in this book or treated as a trunk-trail, end-to-end route of 36 miles. To tour the entire bikeway round-trip from either Erastus Corning Riverfront Preserve in Albany or the northern end at Rotterdam Junction—a 72-mile excursion—would be beyond the ability or interest of most fat-tire day-trippers. It is within reason, however, for the average, in-shape touring cyclist and hybrid rider (or iron-man mountain biker).

169

20

Mohawk-Hudson Bikeway 1: Albany to Watervliet

Location: *Albany, Capitol District*
Terrain: *Flat*
Distance: *10 miles round-trip*
Surface conditions: *Paved*
Maps: *Mohawk-Hudson Bikeway Bike-Hike Trail (available from the Albany County Planning Department, 112 State Street, Albany, NY 12207 with SASE and two stamps); generic Albany/Schenectady/Troy Capitol District map*
Highlights: *State capitol; river views; urban greenbelt and fitness trail; accessible from downtown capitol area*

This section of the Mohawk-Hudson Bikeway tour departs from Albany's Erastus Corning Riverfront Preserve. South of the preserve you can see the historic buildings of the Capitol District. If you follow the bike path a short way, you can access the Albany downtown area from here (under 1 mile). Albany (pop. 101,000) has been the capital of New York since 1797. Named in honor of the Duke of York and Albany, it was first settled in 1614 by the Dutch. It's now an important port because of the connection it provides among the Great Lakes, Canada, and the Atlantic ports.

I recommend a short tour of the downtown area, including the Empire State Plaza, which contains the Cultural Education Center and the award-winning New York State Museum, the Corning Tower Observation Deck, the Legislative Office Building, "The Egg" Performing Arts Center, dozens of shops and eateries, and an underground concourse to the capitol. Capitol-area maps often have insets of the area. Take the Quay Street underpass from the preserve's south end, and head up

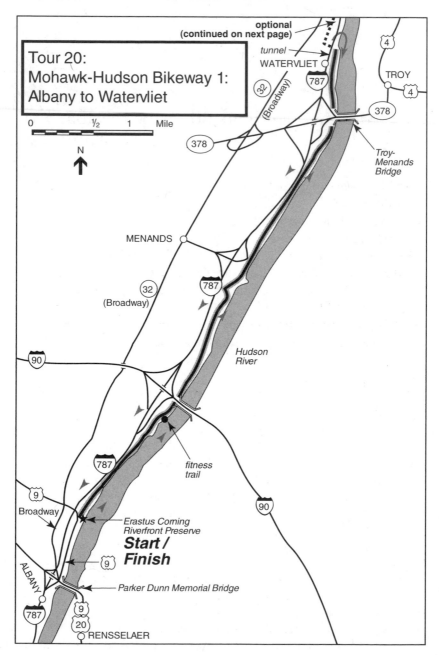

Tour 20:
Mohawk-Hudson Bikeway 1:
Albany to Watervliet

0   ½   1   Mile

N

optional
(continued on next page)
tunnel
WATERVLIET
TROY
787
(32)
(Broadway)
378
4
4
378
Troy-
Menands
Bridge
MENANDS
787
(32)
(Broadway)
Hudson
River
90
787
fitness
trail
90
9
Broadway
*Erastus Corning
Riverfront Preserve*
**Start /
Finish**
9
ALBANY
Parker Dunn Memorial Bridge
787
9
20
RENSSELAER

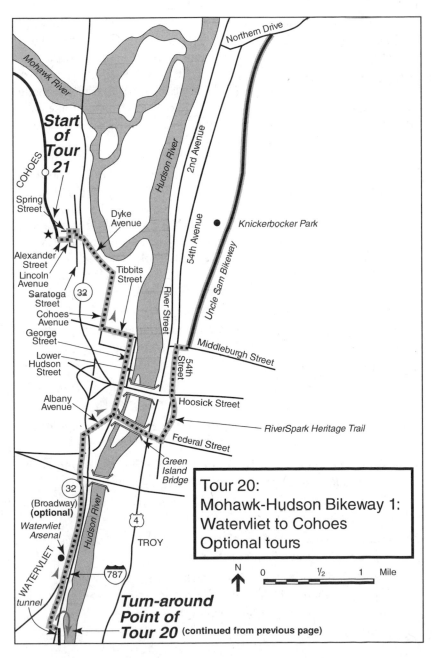

Northern Drive

Mohawk River

Start of Tour 21

COHOES

Hudson River

2nd Avenue

Spring Street

Dyke Avenue

54th Avenue

Knickerbocker Park

Alexander Street
Lincoln Avenue
Saratoga Street

Tibbits Street

32

Uncle Sam Bikeway

River Street

Cohoes Avenue

George Street

Middleburgh Street

Lower Hudson Street

54th Street

Albany Avenue

Hoosick Street

RiverSpark Heritage Trail

Federal Street

Green Island Bridge

**Tour 20:
Mohawk-Hudson Bikeway 1:
Watervliet to Cohoes
Optional tours**

32

(Broadway)
(optional)

Watervliet Arsenal

4

TROY

Hudson River

WATERVLIET

787

tunnel

Turn-around Point of Tour 20 (continued from previous page)

N   0   ½   1   Mile

either Van Zandt, Hamilton, or State Streets to the plaza (0.6 mile). If you can secure your bike, a walk through the complex and a (free) trip up to the observation tower will impress you. (For tourist information, call Empire State Plaza visitors assistance at 518-474-2418.) Bike racks are located on the concourse level of the plaza, and you can bike along the aboveground plaza level, also. If you do plan to leave your bike, take a day pack with you so you can carry your quick-release seat post and accessories. Also, remember to lock both wheels.

To reach the Corning Preserve from the New York State Thruway, take Exit 23 onto I-787 (north). Go approximately 2 miles until you reach US 9 and US 20 where they cross the Parker Dunn Memorial Bridge. Get on US 9 (north), which will bring you to the Corning Preserve at 0.5 mile. Drive slowly (traffic will be pressing you to maintain speed) and watch carefully to your right. You can also reach the preserve from the Quay Street underpass (at the bottom of Broadway in Albany) or the Dunn Memorial Bridge walkway from the Rensselaer side of the Hudson River. There is a large parking lot, many picnic tables, a playground, and rest rooms.

0.00 *To begin the tour from the Corning Preserve, go left (north) on the fitness trail. The Hudson River is to your right.*

0.50 *Pass a public boat launch.*

The trail is about 8 feet wide and close to the river as it passes through a wooded floodplain.

1.00 *Pass through a game field, part of the Erastus Corning Fitness Trail.*

1.30 *Go under the I-90 bridge. You can ride either the paved path or an adjacent cinder service road through this section.*

There are wildflowers, large trees, grass, and some experimental rice paddies along the trail.

2.60 *Pass a (bikable) singletrack that loops back to the trail up ahead. Watch out for pedestrians.*

3.10 *Go through a small picnic area. The forest canopy nearly forms a tunnel over the road here, but it's high up—there are no obstructions or invading vegetation.*

Although you are traveling parallel to US 9, there is a distinctive, sheltered greenbelt and close-up river scenery here.

174

Erastus Corning Riverfront Preserve

4.20 Go under the Troy-Menands Bridge.

4.90 The trail ends. There is public parking here. Return the way you came.

   Through cyclists wishing to connect with the Cohoes-Schenectady section of the bikeway should turn left into the tunnel, then turn right immediately onto Broadway, following these directions (not recommended for children):

0.00 Follow Broadway (NY 32) on a defined bikeway shoulder.

0.70 Pass the Watervliet Arsenal on your left.

2.20 At the intersection of Broadway, Water Street, and Albany Avenue, bear right under I-787 onto Albany Avenue, in the direction of the Green Island Bridge.

2.40 Pass the Green Island Bridge (on your right).

2.50 Bear left onto George Street.

3.30 Pass Paine Street Park on your left, and turn left onto Tibbitts Street.

3.50 Turn right onto Cohoes Avenue.

4.00 Curve diagonally (left) where Cohoes Avenue turns into Dyke Avenue.

4.50 Go directly across the busy (and dangerous) intersection of Dyke Avenue, NY 789, and NY 32, onto Spring Street. Use caution!

4.60 Turn left off Spring Street onto Lincoln Avenue.

4.70 Turn right and go to the top of Alexander Street.

5.00 Access the bikeway from the parking lot, turn right. For directions on this section, see Tour 21.

Two areas in Troy on the east side of the river (accessible by the Green Island Bridge) are worthy of mention. RiverSpark's Heritage Trail is a connection of significant natural and historic sites, and the Uncle Sam Bikeway is a 6-mile round-trip paved bike path. The latter bikeway is named for the Troy butcher, Samuel Wilson, who supplied the Army with meat stamped "U.S." during the War of 1812. He was, allegedly, the original "Uncle Sam." For information regarding this area, write RiverSpark, 251 River

Street, Troy, NY 12180 (518-270-8667). Navigate the area with the suggested Mohawk-Hudson Bikeway map.

Bicycle Repair Services

Steiner's Sports
329 Glenmont Road, Glenmont, NY
518-427-2406

The Down Tube Cycle Shop
466 Madison Avenue, Albany, NY
518-434-1711

Klarsfeld's Cyclery & Fitness
1370 Central Avenue, Colonie, NY
518-459-3272

21

Mohawk-Hudson Bikeway 2: Cohoes to Schenectady

Location: *Albany and Schenectady Counties*
Terrain: *Mostly flat, with one major incline*
Distance: *40 miles round-trip*
Surface conditions: *Paved path with limited street detours*
Maps: *Mohawk-Hudson Bikeway Bike-Hike Trail (available from the Albany County Planning Department, 112 State Street, Albany, NY 12207, with SASE and two stamps); generic Albany/Schenectady/Troy Capitol District map*
Highlights: *Rural, suburban commuter path; scenic views of the Mohawk River; extended exercise and training path; all ability levels*

Those who have found outings of over 20 miles either scarce or excessive now have the chance to indulge or outdo themselves. Paved miles are much easer than equal level distances on any broken surface, and this middle section of the Mohawk-Hudson Bikeway is almost completely paved. Wide-tire bikes weren't designed for pavement, nor will some purists (openly) commit themselves to the stuff. More and more, however, urban and rural bikers alike are discovering the dual nature of the street-fighting, all-terrain bicycle: It is fully at home around the curbs, potholes, sewer-drain grid covers, and city rubble that impose themselves on most paved bike routes.

In addition to the hiatus your backside and upper body will enjoy on this tour, it will still give you the scenery and freedom of a day spent outdoors, in a healthful pursuit, where friends and family members of any ability level can accompany you. Only this time you'll have 40 miles of it. You are not obliged, of course, to cover the entire 40 miles. Although you'll find that extended off-road pavement touring (without the

179

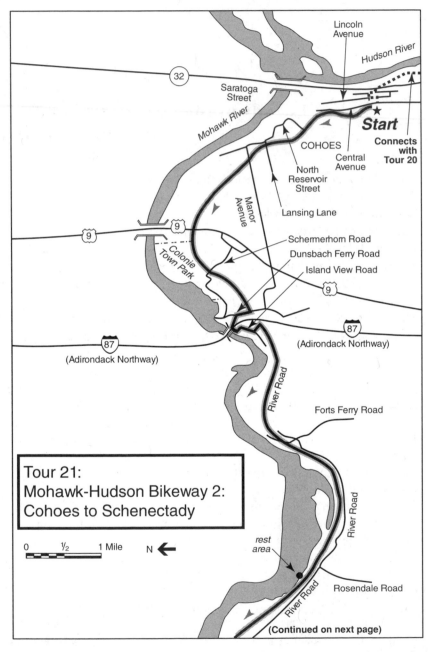

Lincoln Avenue

Hudson River

32

Saratoga Street

Mohawk River

★ **Start**

COHOES

Connects with Tour 20

Central Avenue

North Reservoir Street

Lansing Lane

Manor Avenue

9

9

Colonie Town Park

Schermerhorn Road

Dunsbach Ferry Road

Island View Road

9

87

(Adirondack Northway)

87

(Adirondack Northway)

River Road

Forts Ferry Road

**Tour 21:
Mohawk-Hudson Bikeway 2:
Cohoes to Schenectady**

0   ½   1 Mile   N ←

River Road

rest area

River Road

Rosendale Road

River Road

(Continued on next page)

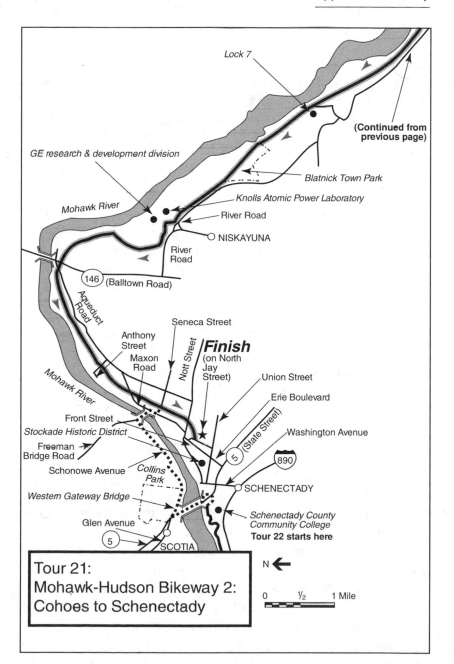

Lock 7

(Continued from previous page)

GE research & development division

Blatnick Town Park

Knolls Atomic Power Laboratory

Mohawk River

River Road

O NISKAYUNA

River Road

(146) (Balltown Road)

Aqueduct Road

Seneca Street

Anthony Street

Maxon Road

Nott Street

Finish
(on North Jay Street)

Union Street

Erie Boulevard

Mohawk River

Front Street

Stockade Historic District

Freeman Bridge Road

Schonowe Avenue

Collins Park

(State Street)

Washington Avenue

5 (State Street)

890

SCHENECTADY

Western Gateway Bridge

Glen Avenue

5

SCOTIA

Schenectady County Community College
Tour 22 starts here

Tour 21:
Mohawk-Hudson Bikeway 2:
Cohoes to Schenectady

N ←

0   ½   1 Mile

distractions of street riding) will enable you to reach new contemplative highs, you can return to reality—and your car—at any point along the trail. Because of this, frequent use of this trail offers excellent fitness advantages: You can gradually increase your mileage and—cautiously—speed, under controlled conditions. If you're so inclined, with today's training aids you can strap on a heart monitor for the tour, return home, download the results into your computer, and, using the appropriate interface hardware and software, graph and analyze your anaerobic threshold (welcome to cyberbiking). For now, all you need is your bike and directions to the trailhead.

For this tour, get off the NYS Thruway at Exit 23, which leads directly onto I-787. If you're coming from the north, take Exit 24 off the NYS Thruway and go east on I-90 until you reach I-787. In either case, go north on I-787 until you reach its intersection with NY 7 (6 miles north of I-90), which you take 0.4 mile west to NY 32 North (Cohoes Road). Go 1.2 miles to the large intersection with Dyke Avenue, and turn left onto Spring Street. Go 0.1 mile up Spring Street, turn left onto Lincoln Avenue, then 0.1 mile to Alexander Street, and turn right. At the top of Alexander Street (0.2 mile), park. Get on your bike and set your odometer to zero.

0.00 *Turn right. The area is residential and peaceful. Go through a huge culvert tunnel.*

1.30 *Go through another culvert.*

1.70 *Cross Lansing Lane.*

North Reservoir Street is to your right. This is the Mohawk River Trailway, Crescent Branch (each township changes the name).

2.00 *Cross Manor Avenue.*

2.50 *There's a brief cinder stretch here. The rural atmosphere increases.*

3.20 *Cross a street, and go through another culvert.*

3.90 *At the path's intersection with Schermerhorn Road, Colonie Town Park is on your right. Here, there are phones, rest rooms, and trail-access parking.*

4.70 *Go right onto a paved road detour (Dunsbach Ferry Road).*

5.00 *Turn left onto Island View Road, crossing under the Adirondack Northway, with the Mohawk River to your right.*

182

5.70 Find the bikeway to your left. Go uphill briefly, then right, downhill.

7.40 Cross Forts Ferry Road.

The trail goes through lush woods.

7.60 Pass a bike path parking area (there are several along this stretch).

7.90 Cross a wooden-plank bridge next to the river.

Mohawk River views are good. There are homes to your left.

Stay on the path.

9.50 Arrive at a rest area at the Niskayuna town line.

11.40 Pass through an area of open fields.

11.80 Arrive at Lock 7.

Here are phones, trail-access parking, picnic sites, a boat launch, and the lock itself, which makes for an interesting rest stop.

13.40 At a Y in the path, you can go either way. Turn left; it's more direct. The trail climbs steeply.

13.60 Pass Woodward Field ballpark (Blatnick Town Park). Bear right. The bikeway goes northwest, adjacent to River Road.

14.20 Pass Knolls Atomic Power Laboratory on your right.

14.80 Pass General Electric's research and development division.

A long downhill through a secluded wooded section follows. (Be careful, there are a couple of hairpin turns.)

17.00 Cross Balltown Road (NY 146), and proceed west, crossing Aqueduct Road into a wooded area.

18.70 Cross Anthony Street into the city of Schenectady.

19.20 Cross Maxon Road.

19.70 Arrive at Seneca Street.

20.50 The trail ends at North Jay Street.

If you're interested, you can tour the shops on North Jay Street or detour down Union Street and Front Street in the Stockade Historic District. Or, you can tack on another 19 miles by crossing the Mohawk off Seneca Street and accessing the Schenectady-to-Rotterdam-Junction section of the bikeway.

There are two ways to reach the trailhead. You can take Seneca Street west to Erie Boulevard, go across the bridge onto Freeman Bridge Road, and turn left onto the bike path. Follow it to Iroquois Street, turn left onto Schonowe Avenue, and turn left again to cross Western Gateway Bridge on NY 5. Turn right after you cross the bridge into the Schenectady County Community College parking area. The trail to Rotterdam Junction starts along the river's south shore.

A faster way to reach the bike path to Rotterdam Junction is to take North Jay Street to Union Street, turn right, go to the end of Union Street to Washington Avenue, and turn left. This will bring you to State Street. Turn right as if you were going to cross the bridge. Take your first right (within 100 yards), go down the hill and under the bridge. The trail starts on your right.

If a 59-mile round-trip is too much, read about this route in the next chapter—Mohawk-Hudson Bikeway 3, Schenectady to Rotterdam Junction—and save it for another day.

Return from wherever you wish.

Bicycle Repair Services

Plaine's
1816 State Street, Schenectady, NY
518-346-1433

Steiner's Sports
329 Glenmont Road, Glenmont, NY
518-427-2406

Mohawk-Hudson Bikeway 3: Schenectady to Rotterdam Junction

Location: Schenectady County, City of Schenectady
Terrain: Gently rolling
Distance: 14 miles round-trip
Surface conditions: Paved
Maps: Mohawk-Hudson Bikeway Bike-Hike Trail (available from the Albany County Planning Department, 112 State Street, Albany, NY 12207, with SASE and two stamps); generic Albany/Schenectady/Troy Capitol District map
Highlights: Scenic views of Mohawk River

Less developed, more secluded, and almost entirely following the Mohawk's wild and overgrown shoreline, this richly scenic and gently rolling trail forms the west end of the Mohawk-Hudson Bikeway. A good place to rendezvous or begin the journey with a group of people is Collins Park in Scotia. Collins Park is on the north side of the river, immediately across the bridge connecting Scotia to Schenectady (the trail begins on the Schenectady side). The park has comfort stations, a picnic area, and a beach area.

The most convenient place to begin, though, is at the trailhead, which starts on the south side of the river, from Schenectady County Community College's playing fields. Beginning at Collins Park means first crossing the bridge (Western Gateway Bridge), which has a sidewalk but is not recommended for small children. However, the vantage point over the river is worthwhile—you can see the marshy, low isles of the Cayugas, Onondagas, Senecas, Mohawks, and Oneidas slowly washing away in the pull of the river beyond the clamorous activity of Jumpin' Jack's fast-food restaurant on the north shore (try their fries).

To reach the bikeway from out of town, take I-90 to Exit 25 at I-890. Go 5 miles to Exit 4C. As you exit, get in the center lane. Within 0.1 mile on your left you'll see Schenectady County Community College.

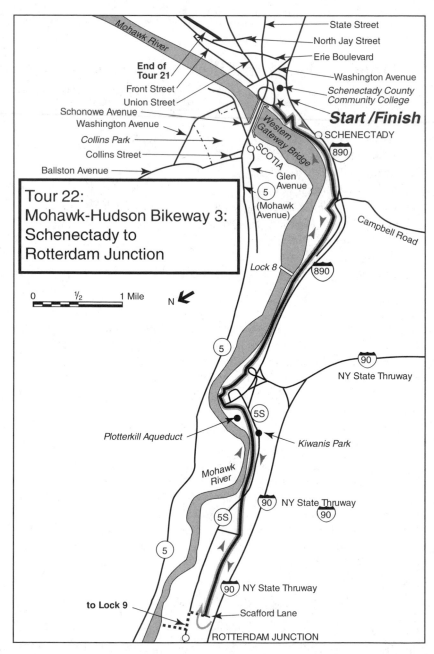

State Street
North Jay Street
Erie Boulevard
Washington Avenue
Schenectady County Community College
End of Tour 21
Front Street
Union Street
Schonowe Avenue
Washington Avenue
Collins Park
Collins Street
Ballston Avenue
Mohawk River
Western Gateway Bridge
Start /Finish
SCHENECTADY
890
SCOTIA
Glen Avenue
5 (Mohawk Avenue)
Campbell Road
Lock 8
890

Tour 22:
Mohawk-Hudson Bikeway 3:
Schenectady to
Rotterdam Junction

0   ½   1 Mile
N

5
90
NY State Thruway

5S
Plotterkill Aqueduct
Kiwanis Park

Mohawk River
90 NY State Thruway 90
5S
5

90 NY State Thruway
to Lock 9
Scafford Lane
ROTTERDAM JUNCTION

186

Immediately past it, go left onto State Street (NY 5). Now you're heading toward Scotia. If you want to go to Collins Park, cross the bridge. The park is on your right. Cross Glen Avenue, the first road on the bridge's west side, and take the first right onto Collins Street and park.

If you're going directly to the trailhead, turn left on State Street and watch for a right turn within 100 yards. This leads to the college parking lots. Go 0.2 mile and under the Western Gateway Bridge. The bikeway starts on the right side of the road, just past the bridge, at the river's edge. There are playing fields here. Park along the road next to the trail.

0.00 Get on the trail, heading west.

1.00 A road merges. This leads to General Electric's water station.

The trailside woods are dense with large cottonwood trees.

2.00 Pass the Campbell Road interchange of I-890.

As you proceed through this area, which follows the Old Erie Canal Towpath, you'll pass Lock 23. Now a ruin, it was made from large limestone blocks.

2.70 Arrive at Lock 8.

This is a good place to picnic and watch boats going through the lock. The lock provides a total lift of 14 feet, from 211 to 225 feet above sea level. Many people bring their families here to relax and watch the river flow. (There is a telephone here.)

After the lock the trail is built on the rockfill of the interstate, and views of the river are inspiring. The path descends into the lush floodplain, weaving through woods.

4.90 Cross the Plotterkill Aqueduct and the old towpath bridge.

5.00 Pass Kiwanis Park picnic area and boat launch.

5.70 Cross NY 5S, and continue on a straightaway adjacent to the canal ditch.

The slack water in the ditch is a disturbing incandescent "green." There are sections of maple swamp along the towpath's left side.

7.00 The path ends at Scafford Lane. Return to your car.

A marked bike path continues from here to cross the river at Lock 9, should you wish to continue. However, as you witnessed at the crossing of NY 5S (5.7-mile mark), this is not a biker-friendly thoroughfare. NY 5S is no place for young riders or those unac-

The bridge at Lock 8, Mohawk River

customed to riding in traffic. Use caution if you choose to use it. *Return the way you came.*

Bicycle Repair Services

Plaine's
1816 State Street, Schenectady, NY
518-346-1433

Steiner's Sports
329 Glenmont Road, Glenmont, NY
518-427-2406

LAKE GEORGE REGION

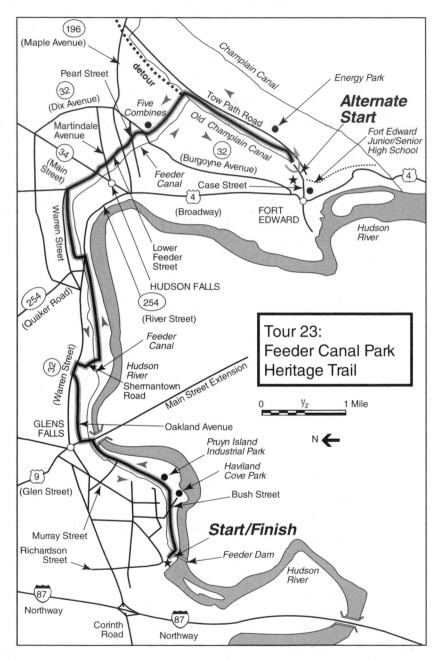

(196)
(Maple Avenue)

Champlain Canal

Energy Park

Pearl Street

detour

(32)
(Dix Avenue)

Five
Combines

Tow Path Road

**Alternate
Start**

Martindale
Avenue

Old Champlain Canal

Fort Edward
Junior/Senior
High School

(34)
(Main
Street)

(32)
(Burgoyne Avenue)

(4)

Warren Street

Feeder
Canal

Case Street

(4)
(Broadway)

FORT
EDWARD

Hudson
River

Lower
Feeder
Street

HUDSON FALLS

(254)
(Quaker Road)

(254)
(River Street)

Feeder
Canal

Tour 23:
Feeder Canal Park
Heritage Trail

(32)

(Warren Street)

Hudson
River

Shermantown
Road

Main Street Extension

0   ½   1 Mile

GLENS
FALLS

Oakland Avenue

N ⬅

(9)
(Glen Street)

Pruyn Island
Industrial Park

Haviland
Cove Park

Bush Street

Murray Street

Richardson
Street

Start/Finish

Feeder Dam

Hudson
River

(87)
Northway

(87)
Northway

Corinth
Road

190

23

Feeder Canal Park Heritage Trail

Location: *Warren County, Glens Falls, and Fort Edward*
Terrain: *Flat*
Distance: *18 miles round-trip*
Surface conditions: *Stone dust, gravel, 4 miles of street detours*
Maps: *Warren County; Glens Falls area*
Highlights: *Linear Heritage Trail; early 1800s canalway; views of Hudson River*

This historical trail is a refined example of what an urban linear park can be. A bikeway, walkway, and commuter and exercise trail, it links the communities of the greater Glens Falls region along the original route of the Glens Falls Feeder Canal.

With its opening in 1822, the Old Champlain Canal joined the extreme south end of Lake Champlain (South Bay) with the Hudson River at Fort Edward, making it possible for boats to travel inland to New York City from the St. Lawrence River. While many people think of Lake Champlain as being north of Lake George, its southern narrows are actually parallel to Lake George's eastern edge. This hydrographic feature has made the canal connection with the Hudson River practical and has enabled trade ships from the St. Lawrence River to reach New York ports via an inland route.

Water from the Hudson at Glens Falls—then called Wing's Falls—was used to fill the canal, and a new dam (to replace an older, flood-damaged one at Fort Edward) was constructed in 1824 to ensure a steady supply. The Feeder Canal is 9 miles long and exists largely intact today.

As well as being an attractive route for land-bound travel, the canal often holds enough water to attract canoeists (paddlers can start at Richardson Street and go about 5 miles east to Martindale Basin).

The effort to preserve and promote the canal's integrity and history is led by the Feeder Canal Alliance (FCA), a nonprofit cultural and educational organization that raises money and sponsors activities such as canal work days, canoe races, and festivals. The FCA has also proposed the development of a Regional Trail that will join the canal path with northern Saratoga County and the Warren County Bikeway. The FCA is interested in seeing the canal path extended into the present-day Champlain Barge Canal and, eventually, to Whitehall. The canal itself and its right-of-way belong to the state of New York and are controlled by the Canal Authority, a branch of the New York State Thruway Department. The FCA also hopes to complete a trail through the town of Moreau, which would form a 14-mile loop back to the Glens Falls Bridge.

To reach the westernmost access point, get off the Adirondack Northway (I-87) at Exit 18. Go east (right if you're traveling north) onto Corinth Road, also called Main Street. Go 0.6 mile and turn right onto Richardson Street, watching carefully for a sign that reads FEEDER CANAL STATE HERITAGE TRAIL. Go another 0.6 mile on Richardson Street until you see the Hudson River (don't go up Haviland Avenue). Park in any of several small, unmarked pull-offs in view of the dam. Signs here indicate the park and trail, which begin along the river's edge.

If you are coming from the east and want to begin in Fort Edward, get on US 4 (accessible from NY 197). US 4 becomes Broadway in Fort Edward and is NY 254 north of town. From Broadway, take Case Street east for 0.2 mile, passing Fort Edward Junior/Senior High School, until you reach the Fort Edward commons and Energy Park. From here, the trail goes northeast, and turns left (west) 1 mile beyond Energy Park's north end.

0.00 **From Richardson Street, walk down to the canal towpath. Go left (east). Signs here read** WELCOME TO FEEDER CANAL PARK.

The canal is to your left. The trail is wide, and views of the river are good here.

0.50 **Cross Bush Street. Following Bush Street will take you to Haviland Cove Park.**

1.10 **Pass Pruyn Island Industrial Park.**

This is a storage yard for Finch Pruyn & Co., Inc. You'll see the mills up ahead. These are probably the biggest log piles you'll ever see.

1.50 Cross Murray Street.
The path assumes an urban atmosphere as you approach Glens Falls.

1.90 Arrive at US 9 (Glen Street).
Cross the street and turn left, riding over the canal and then keeping it to your right, following signs for the canal path. Immediately turn right onto Oakland Avenue. A 1-mile, easy stretch of road is ahead.

2.30 Turn right onto NY 32 (Warren Street).
The smoke-belching stacks of Finch Pruyn are silhouetted by mountains in the background.

2.80 Turn right on Shermantown Road, a dead end.

2.90 Cross over the canal, and turn left to get on the towpath.

3.20 Cross the (private) road leading into the Glens Falls Cement Company grounds.
The canal walls are about 8 feet high along here. Don't get too close, and warn children to stay back. Although the water is shallow, injury is possible.

4.00 Cross NY 254. Continue on the north side.

4.60 Cross Warren Street.

5.50 Arrive at Hudson Falls village. Cross Main Street (US 4) onto Lower Feeder Street. A sign reading FORT EDWARD 2 MILES is on your right.
You'll appreciate the hand-tooled stone canal walls along here.

5.70 Cross Martindale Avenue. This section is paved and residential.

6.10 Cross Maple Avenue (NY 196) and ride back onto a stone-dust surface.

6.20 Cross Pearl Street.

6.60 Cross Burgoyne Avenue. There's an excellent view of the hilly farmland around Hartford, New York, to the east.
The locks begin here, culminating in the "Five Combines," which lower the elevation radically in Kingsbury. There were 13 locks in total, to compensate for the 130-foot vertical drop from Sandy Hill (Hudson Falls).

These locks are in remarkably good condition. The large mound you see to your left is not a historic berm or early fort foundation, but a capped landfill.

6.78 *The "Five Combines" end.*

7.30 *Cross a bridge over the Old Champlain Canal.*

This is the "T" bridge—the last lock. There's a 1.5-mile unpaved detour to your left here, which currently ends at Bond Creek.

Turn right.

8.10 *The path joins a paved road, Tow Path Road, and passes a farm on your left.*

8.50 *A gravel path follows the road.*

9.00 *The trail ends at Energy Park, called McIntyre Park locally.*

Here there are tennis courts, playing fields, and a small pond. Town (Fort Edward) is a few blocks to the west. Return the way you came.

Bicycle Repair Services

Rick's Bike Shop
368 Ridge Road, Queensbury, NY
518-793-8986

Information

Feeder Canal Alliance
PO Box 2414, Glens Falls, NY 12801
518-792-5363

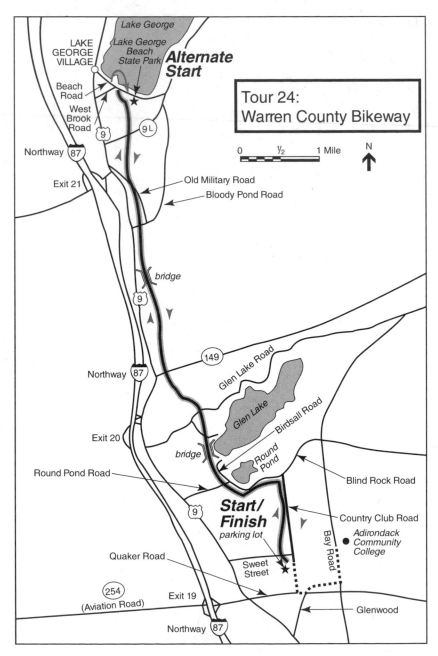

LAKE GEORGE VILLAGE

Lake George

Lake George Beach State Park

Alternate Start

Beach Road

West Brook Road

Northway 87

Exit 21

9

9 L

**Tour 24:
Warren County Bikeway**

0   ½   1 Mile

N

Old Military Road

Bloody Pond Road

bridge

9

149

Glen Lake Road

Northway 87

Glen Lake

Birdsall Road

Exit 20

bridge

Round Pond

Round Pond Road

Blind Rock Road

9

**Start/
Finish**
parking lot

Country Club Road

Bay Road

Adirondack Community College

Quaker Road

Sweet Street

254
(Aviation Road)

Exit 19

Glenwood

Northway 87

196

24
Warren County Bikeway

Location: *Warren County, connecting Glens Falls and Lake George*
Terrain: *Gently rolling*
Distance: *14.8 miles round-trip*
Surface conditions: *Paved bikeway, minimal road travel*
Map: *Warren County Bikeway Area Map (available from Warren County Parks and Recreation Division, Department of Public Works, Warrensburg, NY 12885, 518-623-4141)*
Highlights: *Mountain scenery; woodlands; Lake George Beach State Park; ideal beginner route*

Warren County cyclists, or visitors exploring the extensive scenic rides in the area, will find a variety of routes suited to all ability levels. In addition to attractive county roads, both off-road and touring groups can ride the Prospect Mountain Veterans Memorial Highway to the summit (2021 feet)—a serious workout with a big scenic payoff—and mountain bikers can ride the undeveloped trails around Shelving Rock, Silver Bay, Jabe Pond, and Northwest Bay. Glens Falls has its Feeder Canal Park and bike route, which can be enjoyed by both mountain and touring cyclists (see Tour 23).

But one of the most attractive and accessible bikeways of the region—suitable for any bike and ability level—is the Warren County Bikeway. Rated a beginner route because it is paved and gently contoured, the trail has attributes any cyclist would appreciate. Campers from Lake George, toting tag-alongs and child seats; pedestrians with baby joggers; and neighborhood kids on foot and bikes comprise most of its users. If you start in Glens Falls, this is the ultimate ride-to-the-beach tour; it's the ideal break from camp for those vacationing in Lake George. The up-and-back tour of just under 15 miles can be managed in 2 easy hours.

197

To reach the bikeway from Glens Falls, get off the Adirondack Northway (I-87) at Exit 19. Turn east (right, if you're heading north) on Aviation Road (NY 254). At 0.6 mile, cross US 9. Aviation Road becomes Quaker Road. Continue east on Quaker Road for 0.6 mile, turn left on Country Club Road, go 0.3 mile, and park at the Warren County Bike Path parking area. There are a few picnic tables in this wooded lot.

0.00 *Head north (right) on the bike path.*

If you were to turn left, you would find the trail continues in a southeasterly direction before turning north to Adirondack Community College.

0.25 *Cross Sweet Street through a set of wooden barriers.*

Slow down for pedestrians. This is a residential area.

0.70 *Turn left at a road crossing.*

This is a short section of busy road, but there are good shoulders and markings. Ride on the right.

1.30 *Turn left at the intersection of Blind Rock Road and Round Pond Road.*

2.00 *Go right on Birdsall Road, leaving Round Pond to your right.*

2.34 *As Birdsall Road bends around into the east, go left on the bike path.*

This section is wooded and quiet.

2.70 *Cross a wooden bridge and the outlet of Glen Lake.*

There are views of the Luzerne Mountains from here, beyond Glen Lake swamp. From north to south: Darling, 1850 feet; Bucktail, 1837 feet; Bartlett, 1540 feet.

2.80 *Enter the woods on the north side of Glen Lake Road.*

3.80 *Cross over NY 149.*

The path enters a pine forest over gently rolling terrain. A small picnic area is to your right beyond this point.

5.50 *Emerge from the woods at US 9 and follow the bike path north.*

Several outlet malls exist immediately to the south, on US 9.

5.60 *Cross Bloody Pond Road. A long downhill follows.*

The Warren County Bikeway crosses Glen Lake Outlet.

6.30 *Ride a short stretch (0.1 mile) of the Old Military Road and reenter the woods.*

6.90 *Cross over NY 9L (American Legion Drive).*

7.40 *Arrive at Lake George Battleground State Historic Site and Lake George Beach State Park (called the Million Dollar Beach, because of the view).*

The view from this point *is* impressive—a 35-mile panorama of six lakes and mountains to the north. Peaks in excess of 2000 feet are numerous to the east. There are several lower peaks to the north beyond North Bolton and Northwest Bay. Prospect Mountain is to the west (left).

The trail officially ends (or begins) at West Brook Road and is identified by a large sign. For those accessing the trail from Lake George Village, this is directly south of the beach, where West Brook Road intersects with Beach Road.

Though the tourist appeal of the town itself is overwhelming, a ride through the streets among the many eateries and souvenirs shops is an experience. Contact the local chamber of commerce or stop at the information booth at Blais Lakefront Park (left on Beach Road; there are phones and rest rooms here) for a list of local highlights and activities.

Return the way you came.

Bicycle Repair Services

Rick's Bike Shop
368 Ridge Road, Queensbury, NY
518-793-8986

Information

Warren County Parks and Recreation
4028 Main Street, Warrensburg, NY 12885
518-623-2877

25

Hudson River Recreation Area

Location: Lake Luzerne, Warren County; access from Glens Falls
Terrain: Flat to hilly
Distance: 15.6 miles in two separate circuits
Surface conditions: Dirt
Maps: Area maps are handed out on-site, in season. USGS Area
  Topographic Map, Lake Luzerne
Highlights: Scenic dirt roads next to the Hudson River, with opportunities to camp and swim; all levels of difficulty

The Hudson River Recreation Area (HRRA) is bounded along a several-mile stretch of its western edge by the Hudson River, and you can camp, swim, canoe, fish, picnic, and ride next to the river.

The area is a multiple-use, primitive site (there are no services, phones, flush toilets, or full-time personnel), which was given to the state in 1992 as a result of cooperation with its owner, Niagara Mohawk, and funding from several sources, including the Mellon Foundation and the New York State Conservation Fund. Management and development of the area has been a joint NYS Department of Environmental Conservation and Warren County Parks and Recreation Division effort.

Although small at 1132 acres (it seems much larger), the area has a variety of legal mountain bike trails, which it promotes in the HRRA map and handout available at the entrance gate. There are no parking, camping, or day-use fees. In season, the state maintains a day staff of "river stewards," helpful people who provide orientation, maintenance, interpretive programs, and emergency assistance. They can answer questions about use of the area.

Hikers and equestrians are encouraged to use the HRRA, and do (although evidence of the latter is minimal), but the largest user group

201

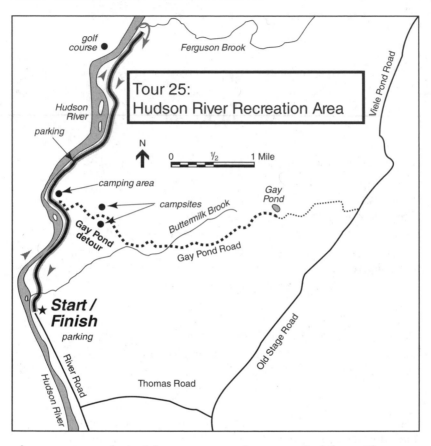

after campers and picnickers appears to be mountain bikers. There are two separate tours, beginner's and advanced, which can conveniently be combined.

A wide range of surfaces and ability levels exist at the HRRA, and on (legal) lands surrounding it. Long stretches of dirt road just outside the entrance follow the river, and loops can be made by connecting trails with roads in some cases. Still more unmapped trails are available for exploration. HRRA represents a transitional atmosphere between the controlled and managed state campgrounds and the more remote wilderness areas. For this reason it's an excellent place for families or beginners wishing to get another step closer to forest bike travel. **Bring adequate provisions, and don't forget insect repellent.**

To reach the area, get off the Northway (I-87) at Exit 18 in South

Glens Falls. Set your trip odometer. Turn west on Corinth Road (County Route 28) toward Lake Luzerne and West Mountain. At 10 miles, at a T, turn right onto County Route 16. Follow this road until reaching an intersection at 14.5 miles. Go straight through this intersection, crossing NY 9N.

The river is on your left as you go into Lake Luzerne village. Continue straight through the village, turning left at the corner of Wall and Main Streets. There are no signs to direct you to the HRRA. If you're lost, ask for directions to River Road (which you can also access from NY 9N if you're heading south). Follow along on River Road through an area of mountainous scenery, with the Hudson River on your left. You'll pass Schofield Road on your right 18.3 miles from the I-87 exit. At 19.7 miles the road turns to dirt. At 21 miles bear left, following close to the river. There are legal camping areas on state land along this stretch. Enter the HRRA at 22.3 miles. Park here.

If you are coming from the north, you can get off I-87 at Exit 19, go west on Aviation Road, turn left at 2.2 miles onto West Mountain Road, and turn right at 4.9 miles onto Luzerne Road (which becomes Glens Falls Mountain Road). At 10.3 miles go right on County Route 16 until you reach the intersection of NY 9N at 12.4 miles. Follow the above directions from this point.

River Road Section, 8+ miles

0.00 *From the main parking area, ride north.*

You start on a well-maintained, wide gravel road. Motor vehicles are permitted on this section, but they'll be traveling slowly. This is an extremely scenic ride. There are many places to pull over next to the river and many unmarked side trails. Don't ride on the nature trails.

1.70 *You'll reach a well-defined Y in the road. To your right is Gay Pond, the advanced route. Bear left, staying on River Road.*

There's a large camping area here in a dense pine forest. There are picnic areas throughout this section, many of them at the river's edge.

2.20 *Pass a parking area next to the river (on your left). Most cars can make it to this area, but no parking is permitted north beyond it.*

3.20 At a Y in the trail, bear left.

Although the road (uphill) to your right looks like a good one that might loop back, it doesn't. It leads in 0.2 mile to a log decking area, which degenerates into several skid trails that are obstructed with ruts, rocks, and slash—the debris left behind from fallen trees. There's a bike route sign here, indicating River Road.

The trail goes through a dense forest, and side trails, most of them marginally ridable skid roads, abound. There are a few different sections that may involve walking.

For beginners, it's not worth going beyond this section of trail, which parallels the golf course visible on the river's west bank. Advanced riders can continue to the confluence of Ferguson Brook.

4.30 Reach Ferguson Brook.

The trail beyond this point is vague and ultimately disappears. A trail uphill to your right is technical and follows Ferguson Brook. It is not recommended, being steep, rocky, and fragile in terms of its vegetation.

River Road is shown on many maps as continuing to Thurman Station, but at this point the trail stops.

Return the way you came.

Gay Pond Detour, 7 miles

More advanced riders will enjoy the Gay Pond trail, a round trip of 7 miles. Begin from the Y at the camping area (at 2.6 miles on your way back from Ferguson Brook, or 1.7 miles from the main gate parking area).

0.00 Begin, heading uphill.

There are several designated campsites along this road.

1.30 Pass the trail to Bear Slide on your right (no bikes). The surface is rocky.

1.60 There is a trail (doubletrack) to the left. Go straight, uphill.

3.50 Bear left, going downhill to arrive at Gay Pond, which is only a few acres in size.

The Hudson River, Hudson River Recreation Area

The trail continues—from where you turned left—out to Old Stage Road and Viele Pond Road. Taking this loop, from Old Stage Road to Thomas Road and back into the HRRA, will add an additional 8 to 10 miles to the tour, a good deal of it on dirt roads. If you don't wish to add the additional mileage, however, you can return the way you came.

One of the amenities of the climb to Gay Pond is that you get to come back almost entirely downhill. Exercise caution.

Bicycle Repair Services

Rick's Bike Shop
368 Ridge Road, Queensbury, NY
518-793-8986

Information

Warren County Parks and Recreation
4028 Main Street, Warrensburg, NY 12885
518-623-2877

Appendix

Resources

Advocacy Groups

Rails to Trails Conservancy
1100 17th Street NW, 10th Floor, Washington, DC 20036

Adventure Cycling Association
150 East Pine Street, PO Box 8308, Missoula, MT 59802
(Expeditions, maps, technical/nutritional advice, advocacy.)

International Mountain Biking Organization
PO Box 7578, Boulder, CO 80306

New York Bicycling Coalition
PO Box 7335, Albany, NY 12224; www.nybc.net
(An excellent source of online information on clubs, events, organizations, routes, maps, books, etc.)

League of American Bicyclists
1612 K Street, NW, Suite 800, Washington, DC 20006

Publications

The Complete Mountain Biker
Dennis Coello, 1989
Lyons & Burford, Publishers
31 West 21 Street, New York, NY 10010

Sloane's Complete Book of All-Terrain Bicycles
Eugene A. Sloane, 1991
Simon & Schuster
1230 Avenue of the Americas, New York, NY 10020

Mountain Biking: The Complete Guide
Sports Illustrated, Winner's Circle Books
Time & Life Building
1271 Avenue of the Americas
New York, NY 10020

Women's Groups and Publications

Women's Mountain Bike and Tea Society (WOMBATS)
PO Box 757, Fairfax, CA 94978
24-hour hotline: 415-459-0980; FAX: 415-459-0832
(Advocacy, workshops, newsletters, national chapters, events.)

Mountain Biking for Women
Robin Stuart and Cathy Jensen, 1994
Acorn Publishing
Waverly, NY 14892

A Woman's Guide to Cycling
Susan Weaver, 1991
Ten Speed Press
Berkeley, CA 94701

Cycling for Women
Editors of *Bicycling Magazine,* 1989
Rodale Press
Emmaus, PA 18049